Shin Buddhist Service Book

Shin Buddhist Service Book

Buddhist Education Center
Orange County Buddhist Church
www.ocbuddhist.org

On the cover: the *myōgō* (名号) or six-character Name

南	無	阿	彌	陀	佛
NA	MO	A	MI	DA	BUTSU

Shin Buddhist
Service Book

Copyright 2013
Corrected second printing, 2014

Published by Buddhist Education Center
Anaheim, California

All rights reserved. No part of this book
may be reproduced without written
permission and consent of the publisher.

ISBN 978-0-9721395-7-1

Printed in the USA

Table of Contents

Entering 1
   Welcome 2
   Coming to the Temple 3
   Temple Customs 3

Speaking 7
   Golden Chain 8
   Shinran's Words 8
   Shin Buddhist Life Principles 9
   Three Treasures 10
   Four Noble Truths 11
   Six Pāramitās 11
   Eightfold Path to Happiness 12
   Selected Sayings 13
   The Tradition of Shinran 20
   White Ashes 21
   Contemporary Readings 22

Chanting 27
   What We Experience by Chanting 28
   Sambujō 29
   Shishinrai 30
   Vandana Tisarana 31
   About the Larger Sutra 32
   Sanbutsuge 33
   Jūseige 39
   Shijūhachigan 44
   About the Jūnirai 48
   Jūnirai 49
   About the Amida Sutra 55
   Amida Sutra 56
   About the Shōshinge 62
   Shōshinge 63
      Gyōfu Style 63
      Sōfu Style 69
      Jūnirai Style 73

Nembutsu Wasan 76
Nembutsu Wasan in English 82
Shōshinge in English Prose.. 83
Shōshinge in English Verse 88

Singing 93
Amida's Gift 94
Amida's Guiding Light 95
Amida's Way 96
Amida's Shrine 98
Asa no Uta 99
Awaken in Amida's Light 100
Buddha Loves You 102
Evening Gatha 103
Falling Leaves 104
Farewell 106
Fundarike 107
Gassho, 'Round the World 108
Hanamatsuri 110
Hanamatsuri no Uta 111
Hanamatsuri Kodomo no Uta 112
Happy Little Children 114
Hotoke no Kodomo 115
Hotoke Sama 116
In Lumbini's Garden 117
I'm a Link in the Golden Chain 118
Infinite Love and Wisdom 120
Listen to His Voice 121
It's Raining.. 122
Joyful in Amida's Light 124
Kiyokeki Hikari 126
Life of Shinran 128
Maru Sankaku Shikaku 130
Mihotoke ni Idakarete 132
Mihotoke wa 133
Minna Nakayoku 134
Nadame 135
Namo Amida Butsu 136
Nembutsu I & II 137

Nichiyobi 138
Nori no Miyama 139
Now We See 140
Obon, Obon, It's Festival Day 142
Okagesama De 143
Ondokusan 144
Ondokusan I 145
Ondokusan II 146
Path of Nembutsu 147
Raisan-ka 148
Right Meditation 150
Sayonara 151
Seiya 152
Shinransama 154
Shinshū Shūka 156
The Texture of Life 157
Thank You Gatha 158
The Chanting of the Sutras 160
To Our Children 162
Tsuki ga Deta 164
Vandana Tisarana 165
When We See the Golden Sun 166
With Grateful Hearts 167
With These Hands 168

Notes 171
   Shinran's Path 172
   Shinran's Teaching 173
   Types of Services and Observances 174
   Special Services 175
   Descriptions of Special Services 176
   Memorial Services 182
   Sources 183

Entering

Welcome

You have come to a Mahāyāna Buddhist temple in the **Jōdo Shinshū** tradition established 800 years ago in Japan by Shinran Shōnin. The words Jōdo Shinshū mean "True Essence of the Pure Land Path." This tradition is often called **Shin Buddhism**.

Twenty-five centuries ago in India, Siddhārtha Gautama searched for a way to transcend the human condition of *duhkha*, which means difficulty, frustration, or suffering. He awakened to the underlying truths of existence: all things are impermanent; dissatisfaction comes from our inability to be one with that truth; we are all interconnected; and oneness with these truths leads to liberation. With this realization he became Śākyamuni Buddha, an awakened human being. His teachings spread throughout Asia in three great streams called Theravāda, Mahāyāna, and Vajrayāna.

Shinran became a Buddhist monk at the age of nine, but after twenty years of dedicated practice he was unable to attain enlightenment. Abandoning that approach, he met his true teacher Hōnen and embarked on the Shin Buddhist path. It is a non-monastic life of deep reflection on human frailty, a life in which the Buddha's Wisdom and Compassion can bring about awakening in the midst of everyday difficulties. This life of awakening is expressed by the word *shinjin*.

Shinran's tradition is the most widespread form of Buddhism in Japan. It was brought to Hawaii and North America in the late 19th century and was sustained initially by Japanese immigrant families. From these roots, it has evolved into a Sangha (a community of Buddhists) having a diverse membership with more than 100 temples in the United States and Canada. The temple is a center of Shin Buddhist life, committed to the inclusion of all people regardless of gender, race, ethnicity, age, disability, sexual orientation, gender identity or expression, or national origin. We welcome all who wish to become a part of our Sangha in following the path of Śākyamuni and Shinran.

Coming to the Temple

A service is a time when Sangha members and friends gather at the temple to listen to the Dharma, our Buddhist teachings. Services include a Dharma talk by the minister and rituals that prepare us to listen to and receive the Dharma. Many of the rituals are performed by the minister and Sangha together. Those who attend are welcome to participate in readings, chanting, singing and offering incense. Except for private weddings, private funerals and memorial observances, temple services are open to everyone.

Temple Customs

The customary practices of the Sangha are based on the reverence and respect we feel for the Three Treasures: Buddha, Dharma, and Sangha. They exist to guide us towards a life of awakening, inner peace, and harmony.

Entering the hondō (main hall) of the temple: When entering or exiting, face the onaijin (altar) and make a slight bow of respect. We are entering the realm of Amida Buddha, the representation of Immeasurable Wisdom and Compassion. We come to the temple to hear the Dharma teachings that will allow us to live each moment with reverence and gratitude.

Onenju and Gasshō: The onenju (or ojuzu) is a circle of beads carried in the left hand or worn on the wrist to remind us of our blind passions. The onenju is treated with respect at all times. Gasshō means to put our palms together with the onenju encircling them.

Before service begins: After being seated in the hondō, it is customary to bow in gasshō and say "Namo Amida Butsu." It is a good opportunity for quiet reflection and meditation.

Nembutsu: We recite "Namo Amida Butsu" while hearing the words as a command to take refuge in Amida Buddha. Nembutsu is our Buddhist life manifested verbally and is also an expression of gratitude for the Buddha, Dharma and Sangha. It is said before and after chanting and after Dharma talks, but it can also be said informally at any time. Other ways of saying the nembutsu are "Namu Amida Butsu," "Namandabutsu," "Namandabu," and "Namandab," which all carry the same meaning.

Kanshō: The "calling bell" or kanshō is struck at the beginning of the service. We can think of it as Amida Buddha, Ultimate Reality, calling us to come and hear the Dharma. Listening to each sound of the bell as it disappears helps us to become reflective and ready to listen.

Oshōkō: An incense offering is made in front of the onaijin. Stand before a burner a few paces away. Bow slightly, and with your left foot first, approach the burner. Take some ground incense with your right hand, and drop it onto the coal. Bow in gasshō, saying the nembutsu, then step back with your right foot, and bow slightly again. Oshōkō may be performed before, during, or at the end of service, depending on temple customs. In Shin Buddhism, offering incense is an expression of reverence and gratitude. It is not done for self-purification or to bring material benefits.

Okesa: The okesa is an embroidered cloth draped around the neck that symbolizes membership in a Buddhist Sangha. It is an emblem of the robes worn by Śākyamuni Buddha and his disciples. The simplified okesa for lay members is called a *monto shikisho*. Wearing it at services is encouraged and indicates readiness to hear the Dharma.

Onaijin: The onaijin is the altar area and represents the Pure Land of Amida Buddha or nirvāna. There are typically five altars on the onaijin, but some temples have three. The central altar in a Shin temple always represents Amida Buddha, in the form of a statue, a painting, or a scroll of Namo Amida Butsu written in Chinese characters. When facing the onaijin, the altar on the right honors the founder of our Shin tradition, Shinran Shōnin. Additional altars will honor notable historical Buddhist figures. Every item on the onaijin is symbolic and represents an aspect of the Dharma.

Osaisen: Monetary offerings are made by donations into osaisen containers either at the back or front of the hondō and reflect the aspect of *Dāna* or giving.

Service Book: The service book contains words of wisdom, and we thus show our reverence by raising the closed book toward our forehead before and after opening and closing it. Out of respect, never lay a service book on the floor.

Speaking

The Golden Chain

I am a link in Amida's golden chain of love that stretches around the world. I will keep my link bright and strong.

May I be kind and gentle to every living thing and protect all who are weaker than myself.

May I think pure and beautiful thoughts, say pure and beautiful words, and do pure and beautiful deeds.

May every link in Amida's golden chain of love be bright and strong, and may we all attain perfect peace.

Shinran's Words

1.
Reverently entrusting myself to the teaching, practice, and realization that are the true essence of the Pure Land way, I am especially aware of the profundity of the Tathāgata's benevolence. Here I rejoice in what I have heard and extol what I have received.

2.
How joyous I am, my heart and mind being rooted in the Buddha-ground of the universal Vow, and my thoughts and feelings flowing within the Dharma-ocean, which is beyond comprehension! I am deeply aware of Tathāgata's immense compassion, and I sincerely revere the benevolent care behind the masters' teaching activity.

3.
The radiant light, unhindered and inconceivable, eradicates suffering and brings realization of joy; the excellent Name, perfectly embodying all practices, eliminates obstacles and dispels doubt. This is the teaching and practice for our era; devote yourself solely to it.

4.
When on board the ship of the great compassionate Vow, let pure shinjin be the favorable wind, and in the dark night of ignorance, let the jewel of virtue be a great torch. Those whose minds are dark and whose understanding is deficient, endeavor in this way with reverence! Those whose evils are heavy and whose karmic obstructions are many, deeply revere this shinjin!

5.
When, through Amida's directing of virtue to them by the power of the Vow, the foolish beings ever floundering in birth-and-death hear the true and real virtues and realize supreme shinjin, they immediately attain great joy and reach the stage of non-retrogression, so that without being made to sunder their blind passions, they are brought quickly to the realization of great nirvāna.

From *The Collected Works of Shinran*, Vol. 1, © 1997 Jōdo Shinshū Hongwanji-ha, pp. 4, 291, 295, 303, 317.

Shin Buddhist Life Principles

Entrusting in the Vow of the Buddha,
Calling out the Buddha's Name,
I will pass through the journey of life with strength and joy.

Revering the Light of the Buddha,
Reflecting upon my imperfect self,
I will strive to live a life of gratitude.

Following the Teachings of the Buddha,
Discerning the Right Path,
I will share the True Dharma with all.

Rejoicing in the Compassion of the Buddha,
Respecting and aiding all sentient beings,
I will work towards the welfare of society and the world.

Three Treasures

Leader:

How rare and wondrous it is to have been born into human life, and now I live it. How rare and wondrous it is to be able to listen to the Buddha-Dharma, and now I am able to hear it. If I do not transcend the world of delusion in this life, when will I ever attain spiritual liberation? May I, along with the entire Sangha, with sincere heart and mind, rely on that which can be truly relied on in life – the Three Treasures.

All:

I rely on the Buddha. May I, along with all sentient beings, awaken to the Great Path with my entire being and discover the highest aspiration, which is to become a Buddha.

I rely on the Dharma. May I, along with all sentient beings, deeply reflect on the meaning of the sutras and gain wisdom that is as deep and vast as the ocean.

I rely on the Sangha. May I, along with all sentient beings, become one Sangha of life, able to move forward and live with a dynamic spirit that is hindered by nothing.

Leader:

The unsurpassed, deep, and wondrous Dharma, even in millions of kalpas, is extremely difficult to encounter, but now I am able to experience and embrace it. May I come to understand and revere the true meaning of the Tathāgata.

Four Noble Truths

Leader: *All:*

Duhkha – Difficulty	Dissatisfaction comes from not living in accord with the truth of impermanence and interdependence.
Samudāya – Arising	The delusion of self-importance, expressed through greed and anger, is the cause of *duhkha*.
Nirodha – Cessation	The transformation of greed, anger, and delusion is the cure for *duhkha*.
Mārga – Path	Śākyamuni Buddha taught the Eightfold Path as medicine for putting an end to *duhkha*.

Six Pāramitās

Leader: *All:*

Dāna – Giving	May I be generous and helpful.
Śīla – Guidance	May I be guided by the Buddhist precepts.
Ksānti – Tolerance	May I regard the mistakes of others with sympathy.
Vīrya – Perseverance	May I do my best in all things.
Dhyāna – Meditation	May I reflect deeply on my life through the Buddha's teachings.
Prajñā – Insight	May I understand the meaning of Namo Amida Butsu.

Eightfold Path to Happiness

Leader:

The teachings of the Buddha help us to understand the oneness of all life. To lead us in the right direction, the Buddha provided us with the Eightfold Path:

All:

Right Views: To keep free of prejudice and superstition and to see the true nature of life.

Right Thoughts: To turn our minds away from violence and hatred.

Right Speech: To refrain from harmful talk and to use our words wisely.

Right Conduct: To see that our deeds come from peace and goodwill. To grow every day in the Buddha's teachings.

Right Livelihood: To try to earn our living in such a way that we avoid causing suffering.

Right Energy: To use our energies to promote the overcoming of ignorance and destructive desires.

Right Mindfulness: To cherish a good mind, for all that we think and do has its roots in the mind.

Right Meditation: To study the teachings of the Buddha and to practice them to the best of our abilities.

Leader:

May the presence of the Buddha, who said that he would live in his teachings, be our guide. May we follow this path until we, too, realize nirvāna.

Selected Sayings

1.
"He abused me, he laughed at me, he struck me." Thus one thinks, and so long as one retains such thoughts, one's anger continues. Anger will never disappear so long as there are thoughts of resentment in the mind. Anger will disappear just as soon as thoughts of resentment are forgotten.
– *Dhammapada*

2.
To be foolish and to recognize that one is a fool, is better than to be foolish and imagine that one is wise. So long as a man cannot control his own mind, how can he get any satisfaction from thinking such thoughts as, "This is my son" or "This is my treasure"? A foolish man suffers from such thoughts.
– *Dhammapada*

3.
Happiness follows sorrow, sorrow follows happiness, but when one no longer discriminates between happiness and sorrow, a good deed and a bad deed, one is able to realize freedom.
– *Dhammapada*

4.
The secret of health for both mind and body is not to mourn for the past, not to worry about the future, and not to anticipate troubles, but to live wisely and earnestly for the present.
– *Dhammapada*

5.
He who is influenced by likes and dislikes cannot rightly understand the significance of circumstances and tends to be overcome by them; he who is free from attachments rightly understands circumstances, and to him all things become new and significant.
– *Dhammapada*

Dhammapada verses are from *The Teaching of Buddha*, Bukkyō Dendō Kyōkai, Tokyo.

6.
Therefore, be a lamp unto yourself; be a refuge to yourself. Take yourself to no external refuge. Hold fast to the Truth as a lamp; hold fast to the Truth as a refuge. Look not for a refuge in anyone beside yourself.
    – Śākyamuni Buddha's Deathbed Address

7.
Do not seek to know Buddha by his form and attributes; for neither the form nor attributes are the real Buddha. The true Buddha is Enlightenment itself.
    – Avatamsaka Sutra

8.
All existing things are impermanent and without abiding self. They are like the moon reflected in water, like lightning, like shadows, like dew. "The Dharma cannot be expressed by words," the Buddha proclaimed. Thus I bow in reverence to the Noble One, Amida.
    – Jūnirai

9.
The notion of emptiness engenders Compassion. Compassion does away with the distinction between self and other. When one sees the illusory nature of all beings, there is born True Compassion.
    – Donran

10.
Let us cease from wrath, and refrain from angry looks. Nor let us be resentful when others differ from us. For all beings have hearts, and each heart has its own leanings. Their right is our wrong, and our right is their wrong. We are not unquestionably sages, nor are they unquestionably fools. We are both simply ordinary beings. How can anyone lay down a rule by which to distinguish right from wrong? For we are all, one with another, wise and foolish, like a ring which has no end.
    – Shōtoku Taishi

11.
The lotus flower
Is not stained by the mud;
This dewdrop form,
Alone, just as it is,
Manifests the real body of truth.
 – *Ikkyū*

12.
To study the Buddha way is to study the self. To study the self is to forget the self. To forget the self is to be actualized by myriad things.
 – *Dōgen Zenji*

13.
Not pronouncing the nembutsu
There is neither the Buddha nor myself,
Ah, that is truly Namo Amida Butsu.
 – *Bunan Zenji*

14.
There is no place the moon does not shine
But it only illuminates
In the heart of those who gaze at it.
 – *Hōnen Shōnin*

Excerpt from *A Raft From The Other Shore*, ISBN: 4-88363-329-2, by Sho-On Hattori. Copyright © 2000 Jodo Shu Press. All rights reserved. Reprinted by permission of Jodo Shu Press.

15.
Know that the Primal Vow of Amida makes no distinction between people young and old, good and evil; only shinjin is essential. For it is the Vow to save the person whose karmic evil is deep and grave and whose blind passions abound.
 – *Shinran Shōnin (Tannishō 1)*

16.
The nembutsu, for its practicers, is not a practice or a good act. Since it is not performed out of one's own designs, it is not a practice. Since it is not good done through one's own calculation, it is not a good act. Because it arises wholly from Other Power and is free of self-power, for the practicer, it is not a practice or a good act.
– *Shinran Shōnin (Tannishō 8)*

17.
The person who attains shinjin and joy
It is taught, is equal to the Tathāgatas.
Great shinjin is itself Buddha-nature;
Buddha-nature is none other than Tathāgata.
– *Shinran Shōnin (Jōdo Wasan 94)*

18.
For evil sentient beings of wrong views and arrogance,
The nembutsu that embodies Amida's Primal Vow
Is hard to accept in shinjin;
This most difficult of difficulties, nothing surpasses.
– *Shinran Shōnin (Shōshinge)*

19.
I know nothing at all of good or evil. For if I could know thoroughly, as Amida Tathāgata knows, that an act was good, then I would know good. If I could know thoroughly, as the Tathāgata knows, that an act was evil, then I would know evil. But with a foolish being full of blind passions, in this fleeting world – this burning house – all matters without exception are empty and false, totally without truth and sincerity. The nembutsu alone is true and real.
– *Shinran Shōnin (Tannishō Postscript)*

20.
My eyes being hindered by blind passions,
I cannot perceive the light that grasps me;
Yet the great compassion, without tiring,
Illumines me always.
– *Shinran Shōnin (Kōso Wasan 95)*

21.
When we say Namo Amida Butsu,
The countless Buddhas throughout the ten quarters,
Surrounding us a hundredfold, a thousandfold,
Rejoice in and protect us.
– *Shinran Shōnin (Jōdo Wasan 110)*

22.
Those who deeply entrust themselves
To Amida's Vow of great compassion
Should all say Namo Amida Butsu constantly,
Whether they are waking or sleeping.
– *Shinran Shōnin (Shōzōmatsu Wasan 54)*

23.
If one walks looking far ahead and pays no attention to the ground beneath his feet, he will stumble. If one gazes critically upon others and forgets to look into himself, he will bring tragedy upon himself.
– *Rennyo Shōnin*

24.
Hard is the rock, soft the water; yet water wears away the rock. There is an old saying that if there is a will, even the attainment of Buddhahood is possible. No matter how little faith one possesses, if he listens earnestly to the teachings, he will attain faith through the Compassion of the Buddha. Therefore it is important that one listen earnestly to the teachings.
– *Rennyo Shōnin*

25.
The faults of others are easy to see, but our own faults are difficult to recognize. If one sees that he has a fault, he must realize that the fault must be very grave indeed for him to recognize it himself; thus, he must take steps to correct his fault. Because it is difficult for us to see many of our faults, we should listen to the advice of others.
– *Rennyo Shōnin*

26.
There are those who listen to the teachings with the purpose of showing off their knowledge to others, but few are those who listen for the sake of attaining awakening. Those who hear that the Pure Land is a place of pleasure and thus desire rebirth there shall not attain the Supreme Enlightenment. Only those who place their being in Amida Buddha shall attain Buddhahood.
    – *Rennyo Shōnin*

27.
From the standpoint of endowed trust, one should listen to the teaching as if for the first time, even though it has been heard before. People want to hear new and interesting things all the time, but no matter how often one listens to the teaching, one should hear it as if it were a rare, first occasion.
    – *Rennyo Shōnin*

28.
Listen to the Buddhist teaching, even if you must take time out from your daily business. To believe that you will listen when you have some spare time is shallow thinking. There is no tomorrow in listening to the teaching.
    – *Rennyo Shōnin*

29.
The essential teaching of the Buddha Dharma is non-ego. There should be no egoistic attachment to "I." But no one believes that he or she is attached to ego; such a person, however, will be reproached by Shinran Shōnin. Rennyo thus urged us to entrust ourselves to Other Power wherein no ego-self exists.
    – *Rennyo Shōnin (Goichidai Kikigaki)*

30.
Saichi has nothing – which is joy. Outside this there's nothing. Both good and evil – all is taken away. Nothing is left. To have nothing – this is the release, this is the peace. All is taken away by the "Namo Amida Butsu"; this is truly the peace. "Namo Amida Butsu."
    – *Asahara Saichi*

31.
We speak of the Buddha, the Dharma and the Sangha as though they are three different things, but they are really only one. Buddha is manifested in his Dharma and is realized by the Sangha. Therefore, to believe in the Dharma and to cherish the Sangha is to have faith in the Buddha, and to have faith in the Buddha means to believe in the Dharma and to cherish the Sangha. Therefore, people are emancipated and enlightened simply by having faith in the Buddha.
  – *The Teaching of Buddha, Bukkyō Dendō Kyōkai, Tokyo*

32.
The mind of faith is the mind of sincerity; it is a deep mind, a mind that is sincerely glad to be led to Buddha's Pure Land by his power. Therefore, Buddha gives a power to faith that leads people to the Pure Land, a power that purifies them, a power that protects them from self-delusion. Even if they have faith only for a moment, when they hear Buddha's name praised all over the world, they will be led to his Pure Land.
  – *The Teaching of Buddha, Bukkyō Dendō Kyōkai, Tokyo*

33.
One should never forget that it is not because of one's own compassion that one has awakened shinjin, but because of the Buddha's compassion which long ago threw its pure light of shinjin into human minds and dispelled the darkness of their ignorance.
  – *The Teaching of Buddha, Bukkyō Dendō Kyōkai, Tokyo*

34.
The mind of shinjin is pure and gentle, always patient and enduring, never arguing, never causing suffering to others but always pondering the three treasures: the Buddha, the Dharma and the Sangha. Thus happiness spontaneously arises in our minds, and the light for Enlightenment can be found everywhere.
  – *The Teaching of Buddha, Bukkyō Dendō Kyōkai, Tokyo*

The Tradition of Shinran

What is taught in the tradition of Shinran Shōnin is that the entrusting heart is essential. For when we abandon various practices and take refuge in Amida with singleness of heart, our birth in the Pure Land is settled by the Buddha through the inconceivable Vow-Power. The state we thus attain is described as "with awakening of a single thought of entrusting, we join those who are in the stage of the truly settled." Recitation of the nembutsu thereafter should be understood to be the nembutsu as an expression of gratitude for the Tathāgata's benevolence for settling our birth in the Pure Land.
  – *Rennyo Shōnin (Gobunshō)*

White Ashes

In silently contemplating the transient nature of human existence, nothing is more fragile and fleeting in this world than the life of man. Thus, we have not heard of human life lasting for ten thousand years. Life swiftly passes, and who among men can maintain his form for even a hundred years? Whether I go before others, or others go before me; whether it be today, or whether it be tomorrow; who is to know? Those who leave before us are as countless and as fragile as the drops of dew. Though in the morning we may have radiant health, in the evening we may be white ashes.

When the winds of impermanence blow, our eyes are closed forever; and when the last breath leaves us, our face loses its color. Though loved ones gather and lament, everything is of no avail. The body is then sent into an open field and vanishes from this world with the smoke of cremation, leaving only the white ashes. There is nothing more real than this truth of life.

The fragile nature of human existence underlies both the young and the old, and therefore, we must – one and all – turn to the Teaching of the Buddha and awaken to the ultimate source of life. By so understanding the meaning of death, we shall come to fully appreciate the meaning of this life which is unrepeatable and thus to be treasured above all else. By virtue of True Compassion, let us realize the unexcelled value of our human existence; and let us live with the nembutsu, Namo Amida Butsu, in our hearts.

– *Rennyo Shōnin (Gobunshō)*
A Translation by Rev. Taitetsu Unno

Contemporary Readings

Taking Refuge (The Three Treasures)

I take refuge in the Buddha, the one who shows me the way in this life.
I take refuge in the Dharma, the way of understanding and of love.
I take refuge in the Sangha, the community that lives in harmony and awareness.

Dwelling in the refuge of Buddha, I clearly see the path of light and beauty in the world.
Dwelling in the refuge of Dharma, I learn to open many doors on the path of transformation.
Dwelling in the refuge of Sangha, shining light that supports me, keeping my practice free of obstruction.

Taking refuge in the Buddha in myself, I aspire to help all people recognize their own awakened nature, realizing the Mind of Love.
Taking refuge in the Dharma in myself, I aspire to help all people fully master the ways of practice and walk together on the path of liberation.
Taking refuge in the Sangha in myself, I aspire to help all people build Fourfold Communities, to embrace all beings and support their transformation.
— *"Chanting From the Heart: Buddhist Ceremonies and Daily Practices" (2007) by Thich Nhat Hanh with permission of Parallax Press, Berkeley, California, www.parallax.org.*

Here is the Pure Land

Here is the Pure Land
The Pure Land is here
I smile in mindfulness
And dwell in the present moment
The Buddha is seen in an autumn leaf
The Dharma is a floating cloud
The Sangha body is everywhere
My true home is right here.
– *"Finding Our True Home: Living in the Pure Land Here and Now" (2003) by Thich Nhat Hanh with permission of Parallax Press, Berkeley, California, www.parallax.org.*

Bodhisattva Vows

1.
Beings are numberless, I vow to save them.
Desires are inexhaustible, I vow to end them.
Dharma gates are boundless, I vow to enter them.
Buddha's way is unsurpassable, I vow to become it.
– *San Francisco Zen Center*

2.
The many beings are numberless, I vow to save them.
Greed, hatred, and ignorance rise endlessly, I vow to abandon them.
Dharma-gates are countless, I vow to wake to them.
Buddha's way is unsurpassed, I vow to embody it fully.
– *Diamond Sangha, Hawaii*

Listen

Listen. Listen to the voice of the Dharma.
Listen to the birds, singing in the morning,
the wind sighing in the boughs overhead,
and the roar of the waves on the beach.

Listen to the rain on the roof and the snow falling in the fields.

The Dharma speaks to us through the sounds of the world –
forcefully and eloquently and beautifully.
It speaks of the unending change around us,
the immutable truth of interdependence,
and the peace in nature.
Do we have the ears to hear and listen...?

Listen to the nembutsu in the Hondō.
Listen to the noble silence of the Buddha.

– "The Heart of the Buddha-Dharma" by Rev. Kenryu T. Tsuji

The Essential Meaning of the Meditation Sutra

Firstly, I urge you all to awaken your Bodhi mind and take refuge
   in the Three Treasures.
Priests and laymen of the present day, awaken your Bodhi mind,
   you, who find great difficulty in escaping the delusion of birth
   and death and know not how to rejoice in the Buddha-Dharma.
Awaken your Bodhi mind to Amida's Compassion and leap across
   the swift currents of birth, old age, sickness and death and enter
   Amida's Pure Land.
With Gasshō and Respect show reverence to Amida Buddha.

– Shan-tao, freely translated by Rev. Kenryu T. Tsuji

Eternal Now

In the beginningless, endless flow of time
each life is a mere ripple,
existing only for an instantaneous moment
and disappearing forever.

But each life is a unique experience
with beauty and truth, all of its own
with no identical counterpart in history
and none absolutely the same in the future.

Your life, my life —
is attuned to the rhythm of the cosmos
and to the heartbeat of reality.

Each life exists in the Eternal Now.

Each idea that is thought,
each word that is spoken,
each action that is taken,
changes the whole pattern of the universe
for the universe is interdependent.
Think, speak and act, then,
always in the eternal now
with compassion and understanding
for your own enlightenment
and for the enlightenment of all sentient beings.

– *"The Heart of the Buddha-Dharma" by Rev. Kenryu T. Tsuji*

Loving-Kindness (Metta) Meditation

May all beings be happy and well,
May no harm or difficulties come to them,
May they live in peace and harmony.

May I be happy and well,
May no harm or difficulties come to me,
May I live in peace and harmony.

May my family be happy and well,
May no harm or difficulties come to them,
May they live in peace and harmony.

May my teachers be happy and well,
May no harm or difficulties come to them,
May they live in peace and harmony.

May my friends be happy and well,
May no harm or difficulties come to them,
May they live in peace and harmony.

May strangers be happy and well,
May no harm or difficulties come to them,
May they live in peace and harmony.

May my enemies be happy and well,
May no harm or difficulties come to them,
May they live in peace and harmony.

May all beings be happy and well,
May no harm or difficulties come to them,
May they live in peace and harmony.
– *Palo Alto Buddhist Temple Reading*

Chanting

What We Experience by Chanting

Chanting in Shin Buddhism has a meditative aspect, a ritual aspect, and a learning aspect. The meditative aspect of chanting is the same as the meditative aspect of sitting. Being fully engaged in sitting or in chanting enables us to focus on the present moment. Focusing in this way is helpful before listening to a Dharma message. The meditative aspect of chanting is available even if we do not know the meaning of the words.

Chanting also has a ritual aspect. Rituals bring our views into alignment with a timeless message by re-enacting events or stories that express the Buddhist teachings. In chanting the sutras we maintain a link with the disciples of the Buddha who transmitted these words over the centuries. The ritual aspect includes the feeling of oneness that develops among people who participate.

The learning aspect of chanting comes through listening to the Dharma. True listening takes place when we grasp the meaning of the words. It would be difficult to understand the words solely by chanting an English translation of a Chinese text. Instead, we learn to appreciate the meaning by attending study classes and by becoming familiar with the separate English translations in this service book.

Most Shin Buddhist chants conclude with a verse called *Ekōku* or Directing Virtue to All Beings by the Pure Land teacher, Shan-tao:

Gan ni shi ku doku	I vow that the virtue of this truth
Byō dō se is-sai	Be given equally to all.
Dō ho'n bo dai shin	May they awaken the bodhi mind
Ō jō an rak-koku	And realize the realm of peace and joy.

—

Notation used in chanting texts:
○	indicates when to strike the bell
italics	line is chanted by the leader
<u>underline</u>	duration of syllable is extended

Sambujō (三奉請)

(Three Respectful Callings)

We respectfully welcome Amida Buddha to our temple as we scatter flowers of joy.

We respectfully welcome Śākyamuni Buddha to our temple as we scatter flowers of joy.

We respectfully welcome the Buddhas of all times and places to our temple as we scatter flowers of joy.

Shishinrai (至心礼)

(Bowing with Sincere Mind)

With a sincere mind, bow reverently, and take refuge in the timeless Buddha.
With a sincere mind, bow reverently, and take refuge in the timeless Dharma.
With a sincere mind, bow reverently, and take refuge in the timeless Sangha.

Vandana Ti-Sarana
(Homage and Three Refuges)

Homage to Śākyamuni Buddha, the Blessed One, the Noble One, the Perfectly Awakened One.

> I go to the Buddha for guidance.
> I go to the Dharma for guidance.
> I go to the Sangha for guidance.

About the Larger Sutra

We often chant *Sanbutsuge* and *Jūseige* in Shin Buddhist services. These verses are from the *Larger Sutra of Immeasurable Life*, which was composed in India during the first century CE and translated into Chinese around 400 CE. It is a cornerstone text for Pure Land Buddhism in China and Japan. Shinran esteemed the *Larger Sutra* above all other teachings, and he devoted his life to its propagation.

In this sutra, the disciple Ānanda asks why, on this occasion, does Śākyamuni's face appear so radiant: "The Buddhas of the past, future, and present all think on one another. Is it not also the case that you, the present Buddha, think on all other Buddhas now?" Śākyamuni replies, "Well spoken, Ānanda! ...The question you ask will bring immense benefit; it will enlighten the minds of all devas and human beings."

Ānanda's question leads Śākyamuni to transmit the teaching of nembutsu, or "thinking on all Buddhas," through the story of Dharmākara, a quintessential truth seeker. Upon meeting with a teacher, this seeker awakens the aspiration to become a Buddha. Dharmākara vows to liberate all sentient beings and to create a Buddha-land where his aspiration will be fulfilled. By learning from countless Buddhas over many eons, he realizes limitless wisdom and compassion, and he becomes Amida, the Buddha of Immeasurable Light and Life.

What is the nembutsu teaching? It is to hear the meaning of Namo Amida Butsu, which is to be mindful of the ultimate truth symbolized by Amida. Through listening to the *Larger Sutra* we can awaken the aspiration for Buddhahood and become a truth seeker like Dharmākara.

For an English translation of the *Larger Sutra* with explanatory material, please see *The Three Pure Land Sutras*, Vol. II, © 2009 Jōdo Shinshū Hongwanji-ha.

Sanbutsuge (讃仏偈)

○ ○
Kō gen gi gi
I jin mu goku
Nyo ze en myō
Mu yo tō sha
↓
Nichi gatsu ma ni
Shu kō en nyō
Kai shitsu on pei
Yu nyaku ju moku

Nyo rai yō gen
Chō se mu rin
Shō gaku dai on
Kō ru jip-pō

Kai mon shō jin
Sam-mai chi e
I toku mu ryo
Shu shō ke u

Jin tai zen nen
Sho butsu hō kai
Gu jin jin nō
Ku go gai tai

Mu myō yoku nu
Se son yō mu
Nin-no shi shi
Jin toku mu ryō

Ku kun kō dai
Chi e jin myō
Kō myō i sō
Shin dō dai sen

Gan ga sa butsu
Zai shō hō ō
Ka do shō ji
Mi fu ge datsu ↥

Fu se jō i
Kai nin shō jin
Nyo ze sam-mai
Chi e i jō

Go sei toku butsu
Fu gyō shi gan
Is-sai ku ku
I sa dai an

Ke shi u butsu
Hyaku sen-noku man
Mu ryō dai shō
Shu nyo gō ja

Ku yō is-sai
Shi tō sho butsu
Fu nyo gu dō
Ken shō fu gyaku

Hi nyo gō ja
Sho butsu se kai
Bu fu ka ge
Mu shu setsu do

Kō myō shis-shō
Hen shi sho koku
Nyo ze shō jin
I jin nan ryō

Ryō ga sa butsu
Koku do dai ichi
Go shu ki myō
Dō jō chō zetsu

Koku nyo nai on
Ni mu tō sō
Ga tō ai min
Do datsu is-sai

Jip-pō rai shō
Shin-netsu shō jō
I tō ga koku
Ke raku an-non

Kō butsu shin myō
Ze ga shin shō
Hotsu gan-no hi
Riki shō sho yoku

Jip-pō se son
Chi e mu ge
Jō ryō shi son
Chi ga shin gyō

Ke ryō shin shi
Sho ku doku chū
<u>Ga gyō shō jin</u>
<u>Nin jū fu ke</u> ○

Na man da bu ○
Na man da bu
Na man da bu
Na man da bu
Na man da bu
Na man da bu ○

Gan ni shi ku doku
Byō dō se is-sai
Dō ho'n bo dai shin
Ō jō an rak-koku
○ ○ ○

Sanbutsuge (讃仏偈)
The Larger Sutra of Immeasurable Life
Dharmākara Praises His Teacher

At that time there was a king who, having heard the Buddha's exposition of the Dharma, rejoiced in his heart and awakened the aspiration for supreme, true enlightenment. He renounced his kingdom and throne, and undertook practice as a monk named Dharmākara. Possessed of superior intelligence, courage, and wisdom, he surpassed other people of the world. He went to see Lokeśvararāja Tathāgata, bowed at his feet, circumambulated him three times to the right, knelt down on the ground, and, putting his palms together in reverence, praised the Buddha with the following verses:

Your radiant countenance is majestic,
And your dignity is boundless.
Radiant splendor such as yours
Has no equal.

Even the blazing light of
The sun, moon, and mani-jewels
Is completely hidden and obscured,
And looks like a mass of black ink-sticks.

The countenance of the Tathāgata
Is unequaled in the world;
The great voice of the Perfectly Enlightened One
Resounds throughout the ten quarters.

Your observance of precepts, learning, diligence,
Meditation, and wisdom –
The magnificence of these virtues is peerless,
Excellent and unsurpassed.

Deeply and clearly mindful
Of the ocean of the Dharma of all Buddhas,
You know its depth and breadth,
And reach its farthest end.

Ignorance, greed, and anger
Are completely absent in the World-honored One;
You are a lion, the most courageous of all humans,
Having immeasurable majestic virtues.

Your meritorious accomplishment is vast,
And your wisdom is deep and supreme;
The majestic glory of your light
Shakes the great thousand worlds.

I vow to become a Buddha,
Equal to you, the most honored King of the Dharma,
And to bring sentient beings from birth-and-death
To the final attainment of emancipation.

My practice of giving, self-discipline,
Observance of precepts, forbearance, diligence,
And also meditation and wisdom
Shall be unsurpassed.

I resolve that, when I become a Buddha,
I will fulfill this vow in every possible way,
And to all beings who live in fear
I will give great peace.

Even though there are Buddhas
As many as a thousand million kotis,
Or countless great sages
As many as the sands of the Ganges,

I will make offerings
To all these Buddhas;
Nothing surpasses my determination
To seek the Way steadfastly and untiringly.

Even though there are Buddha-worlds
As many as the sands of the Ganges,
And also innumerable lands
Beyond calculation,

My light shall illumine
All of these lands;
I will make such efforts
That my divine power may be boundless.

When I become a Buddha,
My land shall be the most exquisite;
People there shall be unrivaled and excellent
And my seat of enlightenment shall be beyond compare.

My land shall be like nirvāna,
Being supreme and unequaled.
Out of compassion and pity,
I will bring all to emancipation.

Those who come from the ten quarters
Shall rejoice with pure hearts;
Once they reach my land,
They shall dwell in peace and happiness.

May you, the Buddha, be my witness
And attest to the truthfulness of my resolution.
I have thus made my aspiration;
I will endeavor to fulfill it.

The World-honored Ones in the ten quarters
Have unimpeded wisdom;
May these honored ones
Always know my intentions.

Even if I should be subjected to
All kinds of suffering and torment,
Continuing my practice undeterred,
I would endure it and never have any regrets.

From *The Three Pure Land Sutras*, Vol. II, © 2009 Jōdo Shinshū Hongwanji-ha, pp. 14-17.

Sanbutsuge (讃仏偈)

こう げん ぎ ぎ 光 顔 巍 巍 い じん む ごく 威 神 無 極 にょ ぜ えん みょう 如 是 焔 明 む よ とう しゃ 無 与 等 者 にち がつ ま に 日 月 摩 尼 しゅ こう えん にょう 珠 光 焔 耀 かい しつ おん ぺい 皆 悉 隠 蔽 ゆ にゃく じゅ もく 猶 若 聚 墨 にょ らい よう げん 如 来 容 顔 ちょう せ む りん 超 世 無 倫 しょう がく だい おん 正 覚 大 音 こう る じっ ぽう 響 流 十 方 かい もん しょう じん 戒 聞 精 進 さん まい ち え 三 昧 智 慧	い とく む りょ 威 徳 無 侶 しゅ しょう け う 殊 勝 希 有 じん たい ぜん ねん 深 諦 善 念 しょ ぶつ ほう かい 諸 仏 法 海 ぐ じん じん のう 窮 深 尽 奥 く ご がい たい 究 其 涯 底 む みょう よく ぬ 無 明 欲 怒 せ そん よう む 世 尊 永 無 にん の し し 人 雄 師 子 じん とく む りょう 神 徳 無 量 く くん こう だい 功 勲 広 大 ち え じん みょう 智 慧 深 妙 こう みょう い そう 光 明 威 相 しん どう だい せん 震 動 大 千	がん が さ ぶつ 願 我 作 仏 さい しょう ほう おう 斉 聖 法 王 か ど しょう じ 過 度 生 死 み ふ げ だつ 靡 不 解 脱 ふ せ じょう い 布 施 調 意 かい にん しょう じん 戒 忍 精 進 にょ ぜ さん まい 如 是 三 昧 ち え い じょう 智 慧 為 上 ご せい とく ぶつ 吾 誓 得 仏 ふ ぎょう し がん 普 行 此 願 いっ さい く く 一 切 恐 懼 い さ だい あん 為 作 大 安 け し う ぶつ 仮 使 有 仏 ひゃく せん のく まん 百 千 億 万

Sanbutsuge

無量大聖（むりょうだいしょう）
数如恒沙（しゅにょごうじゃ）
供養一切（くようい っさい）
斯等諸仏（しとうしょぶつ）
不如求道（ふにょぐどう）
堅正不却（けんしょうふぎゃく）
譬如恒沙（ひにょごうじゃ）
諸仏世界（しょぶつせかい）
復不可計（ぶふかげ）
無数刹土（むしゅせつど）
光明悉照（こうみょうしっしょう）
徧此諸国（へんしょこく）
如是精進（にょぜしょうじん）
威神難量（いじんなんりょう）
令我作仏（りょうがさぶつ）

国土第一（こくどだいいち）
其衆奇妙（ごしゅきみょう）
道場超絶（どうじょうちょうぜつ）
国如泥洹（こくにょないおん）
而無等双（にむとうそう）
我当哀愍（がとうあいみん）
度脱一切（どだついっさい）
十方来生（じっぽうらいしょう）
心悦清浄（しんねつしょうじょう）
已到我国（いとうがこく）
快楽安穏（けらくあんのん）
幸仏信明（こうぶつしんみょう）
是我真証（ぜがしんしょう）
発願於彼（ほつがんのひ）
力精所欲（りきしょうしょよく）

十方世尊（じっぽうせそん）
智慧無礙（ちえむげ）
常令此尊（じょうりょうしそん）
知我心行（ちがしんぎょう）
仮令身止（けりょうしんし）
諸苦毒中（しょくどくちゅう）
我行精進（が―ぎょうしょうじ―ん）
忍終不悔。（に―んじゅうふ け―）

南无阿弥陀仏。（な― ま―ん だぶ―）
南无阿弥陀仏
南无阿弥陀仏
南无阿弥陀仏
南无阿弥陀仏
南无阿弥陀仏。

願以此功徳（がんにしくどく）
平等施一切（びょうどうせいっさい）
同発菩提心（どうほつぼだいしん）
往生安楽国（おうじょうあんらっこく）
○○○

Jūseige (重誓偈)

○ ○

Ga gon chō se gan
His-shi mu jō dō
Shi gan fu man zoku
Sei fu jō shō gaku

Ga o mu ryō kō
Fu i dai se shu
Fu sai sho bin gu
Sei fu jō shō gaku

Ga shi jō butsu dō
Myō shō chō jip-pō
Ku kyō mi sho mon
Sei fu jō shō gaku

Ri yoku jin shō nen
Jō e shu bon gyō
Shi gu mu jō dō
I sho ten nin shi

Jin riki en dai kō
Fu shō mu sai do
Shō jo san ku myō
Kō sai shu yaku nan

Kai hi chi e gen
Mes-shi kon mō an
Hei soku sho aku dō
Tsū datsu zen shu mon

Ko so jō man zoku
I yō rō jip-pō
Nichi gatsu shū jū ki
Ten kō on fu gen

I shu kai hō zō
Kō se ku doku hō
Jō o dai shu chū
Sep-pō shi shi ku

Ku yō is-sai butsu
Gu soku shu toku hon
Gan-ne shitsu jō man
Toku i san gai o

Nyo butsu mu ge chi
Tsū datsu mi fu shō
Gan ga ku e riki
Tō shi sai shō son

Shi gan nyak-kok-ka
Dai sen ō kan dō
Ko kū sho ten nin
Tō u chin myō ke ○

Na man da bu ○
Na man da bu
Na man da bu
Na man da bu
Na man da bu
Na man da bu ○

Gan ni shi ku doku
Byō dō se is-sai
Dō ho'n bo dai shin
Ō jō an rak-koku

○ ○ ○

Jūseige (重誓偈)
The Larger Sutra of Immeasurable Life
Dharmākara Reiterates the Vows

I have established the all-surpassing vows
And will unfailingly attain supreme enlightenment.
If these vows should not be fulfilled,
May I not attain perfect enlightenment. [12th Vow]

If, for countless kalpas to come,
I should not become a great benefactor
And save all the destitute and afflicted everywhere,
May I not attain perfect enlightenment. [13th Vow]

When I have fulfilled the Buddha-way,
My name shall pervade the ten quarters;
Should there be any place it is not heard,
May I not attain perfect enlightenment. [17th Vow]

Freed from greed and with deep right-mindedness
And pure wisdom, I will perform the sacred practices
In pursuit of supreme enlightenment
And become the teacher of devas and humans.

Emitting a great light with my majestic power,
I will completely illuminate the boundless worlds;
Dispelling, thereby, the darkness of the three defilements,
I will deliver all beings from suffering and affliction.

Having acquired the eye of wisdom,
I will remove the darkness of blind passions;
Blocking the path to the evil realms,
I will open the gate to the good realms.

When my practice and merits are fulfilled,
My majestic brilliance shall reach everywhere in the ten quarters,
Outshining both the sun and the moon;
Even the heavenly lights shall be hidden and obscured.

For the sake of all beings I will open forth the Dharma-store
And universally bestow its treasure of virtue upon them.
Among the multitudes of beings
I will always preach the Dharma with a lion's roar.

Making offerings to all the Buddhas,
I will acquire all the roots of virtue;
With my vows fulfilled and wisdom perfected,
I will be the hero of the three worlds.

Like your unimpeded wisdom, O Buddha Lokeśvararāja,
My wisdom shall reach everywhere and illuminate all;
May the power of my virtue and wisdom
Be equal to that of yours, O Most Honored One.

If these vows are to be fulfilled,
The great thousand worlds will shake in accord,
And from the sky all the devas
Will rain down rare and wondrous flowers.

As soon as Bhiksu Dharmākara finished speaking these verses, the entire earth shook with six kinds of tremors. The heavens rained down wondrous flowers upon it. There was spontaneous music in the sky, which praised him, saying, "You will unfailingly attain supreme, perfect enlightenment." Hereupon, Bhiksu Dharmākara, fully possessed of these great vows and his mind being sincere and not false, made a supramundane aspiration and earnestly sought to attain nirvāna.

From *The Three Pure Land Sutras*, Vol. II, © 2009 Jōdo Shinshū Hongwanji-ha, pp. 30-31.

Jūseige (重誓偈)

○ ○

我(が)建(ごん)超(ちょう)世(せ)願(がん)
必(ひっ)至(し)無(む)上(じょう)道(どう)
斯(し)願(がん)不(ふ)満(まん)足(ぞく)
誓(せい)不(ふ)成(じょう)正(しょう)覚(がく)

我(が)於(お)無(む)量(りょう)劫(こう)
不(ふ)為(い)大(だい)施(せ)主(しゅ)
普(ふ)済(さい)諸(しょ)貧(びん)苦(ぐ)
誓(せい)不(ふ)成(じょう)正(しょう)覚(がく)

我(が)至(し)成(じょう)仏(ぶつ)道(どう)
名(みょう)声(じょう)超(ちょう)十(じっ)方(ぽう)
究(く)竟(きょう)靡(み)所(しょ)聞(もん)
誓(せい)不(ふ)成(じょう)正(しょう)覚(がく)

離(り)欲(よく)深(じん)正(しょう)念(ねん)
浄(じょう)慧(え)修(しゅ)梵(ぼん)行(ぎょう)

志(し)求(ぐ)無(む)上(じょう)道(どう)
為(い)諸(しょ)天(てん)人(にん)師(し)
神(じん)力(りき)演(えん)大(だい)光(こう)
普(ふ)照(しょう)無(む)際(さい)土(ど)
消(しょう)除(じょ)三(さん)垢(く)冥(みょう)
広(こう)済(さい)衆(しゅ)厄(やく)難(なん)
開(かい)彼(ひ)智(ち)慧(え)眼(げん)
滅(めっ)此(し)昏(こん)盲(もう)闇(あん)
閉(へい)塞(そく)諸(しょ)悪(あく)道(どう)
通(つう)達(だつ)善(ぜん)趣(しゅ)門(もん)
功(こう)祚(そ)成(じょう)満(まん)足(ぞく)
威(い)曜(よう)朗(ろう)十(じっ)方(ぽう)
日(にち)月(がつ)戢(しゅう)重(じゅう)暉(き)
天(てん)光(こう)隠(おん)不(ふ)現(げん)

為(い)衆(しゅ)開(かい)法(ほう)蔵(ぞう)
広(こう)施(せ)功(く)徳(どく)宝(ほう)
常(じょう)於(お)大(だい)衆(しゅ)中(ちゅう)
説(せっ)法(ぽう)師(し)子(し)吼(く)

供(く)養(よう)一(いっ)切(さい)仏(ぶつ)
具(ぐ)足(そく)衆(しゅ)徳(とく)本(ほん)
願(がん)慧(ね)悉(しつ)成(じょう)満(まん)
得(とく)為(い)三(さん)界(がい)雄(お)

如(にょ)仏(ぶつ)無(む)礙(げ)智(ち)
通(つう)達(だつ)靡(み)不(ふ)照(しょう)
願(がん)我(が)功(く)慧(え)力(りき)
等(とう)此(し)最(さい)勝(しょう)尊(そん)

斯(し)願(がん)若(にゃっ)剋(こっ)果(か)
大(だい)千(せん)応(おう)感(かん)動(どう)
虚(こ)空(くう)諸(しょ)天(てーん)人(にーん)
当(とーう)雨(う)珍(ちーん)妙(みょーう)華(けー)。

南(な)无(ま)阿(ん)弥(だー)陀(ぶ)仏(ー)。
南 无 阿 弥 陀 仏
南 无 阿 弥 陀 仏
南 无 阿 弥 陀 仏
南 无 阿 弥 陀 仏
南 无 阿 弥 陀 仏。

願(がん)以(に)此(し)功(く)徳(どく)
平(びょう)等(どう)施(せ)一(いち)切(さい)
同(どう)発(ほつ)菩(ぼ)提(だい)心(しん)
往(おう)生(じょう)安(あん)楽(らっ)国(こく)○○。

Shijūhachigan (四十八願)

○ ○

Bus-setsu mu ryō ju kyō

1.
Setsu ga toku butsu
Koku u ji goku
Ga ki chiku shō sha
Fu shu shō gaku

2.
Setsu ga toku butsu
Koku chū nin den
Ju jū shi go
Bu kyō sam-maku dō sha
Fu shu shō gaku

3.
Setsu ga toku butsu
Koku chū nin den
Fu shis-shin kon jiki sha
Fu shu shō gaku

4.
Setsu ga toku butsu
Koku chū nin den
Gyō shiki fu dō
U kō shū sha
Fu shu shō gaku

5.
Setsu ga toku butsu
Koku chū nin den
Fu shiki shuku myō
Ge shi fu chi
Hyaku sen-noku
Na yu ta
Sho kō ji sha
Fu shu shō gaku

6.
Setsu ga toku butsu
Koku chū nin den
Fu toku ten gen
Ge shi fu ken
Hyaku sen-noku
Na yu ta
Sho buk-koku sha
Fu shu shō gaku

7.
Setsu ga toku butsu
Koku chū nin den
Fu toku ten ni
Ge shi mon
Hyaku sen-noku
Na yu ta
Sho bus-sho setsu
Fu shitsu ju ji sha
Fu shu shō gaku

8.
Setsu ga toku butsu
Koku chū nin den
Fu toku ken ta shin chi
Ge shi fu chi
Hyaku sen-noku
Na yu ta
Sho buk-koku chū
Shu jō shin nen sha
Fu shu shō gaku

9.
Setsu ga toku butsu
Koku chū nin den
Fu toku jin soku
O ichi nen kyō
Ge shi fu nō
Chō ka hyaku sen-noku
Na yu ta
Sho buk-koku sha
Fu shu shō gaku

10.
Setsu ga toku butsu
Koku chū nin den
Nyak-ki sō nen
Ton ge shin sha
Fu shu shō gaku

11.
Setsu ga toku butsu
Koku chū nin den
Fu jū jō ju
His-shi metsu do sha
Fu shu shō gaku

12.
Setsu ga toku butsu
Kō myō u nō gen ryō
Ge shi fu shō
Hyaku sen-noku
Na yu ta
Sho buk-koku sha
Fu shu shō gaku

13.
Setsu ga toku butsu
Ju myō u nō gen ryō
Ge shi hyaku sen-noku
Na yu ta kō sha
Fu shu shō gaku

14.
Setsu ga toku butsu
Koku chū shō mon
U nō ke ryō
Ge shi san zen
Dai sen se kai
Shō mon en gaku
O hyaku sen gō
Shitsu gu ke kyō
Chi go shu sha
Fu shu shō gaku

15.
Setsu ga toku butsu
Koku chū nin den
Ju myō mu nō gen ryō
Jo go hon gan
Shu tan ji zai
Nyaku fu ni sha
Fu shu shō gaku

16.
Setsu ga toku butsu
Koku chū nin den
Nai shi mon-nu
Fu zen myō sha
Fu shu shō gaku

17.
Setsu ga toku butsu
Jip-pō se kai
Mu ryō sho butsu
Fu shis-shi sha
Shō ga myō sha
Fu shu shō gaku

18.
Setsu ga toku butsu
Jip-pō shu jō
Shi shin shin gyō
Yoku shō ga koku
Nai shi jū nen
Nyaku fu shō ja
Fu shu shō gaku
Yui jo go gyaku
Hi hō shō bō

19.
Setsu ga toku butsu
Jip-pō shu jō
Hotsu bo dai shin
Shu sho ku doku
Shi shin hotsu gan

Yoku shō ga koku
Rin ju jū ji
Ke ryō fu yo
Dai shu i nyō
Gen go nin zen ja
Fu shu shō gaku

20.
Setsu ga toku butsu
Jip-pō shu jō
Mon ga myō gō
Ke nen ga koku
Jiki sho toku hon
Shi shin e kō
Yoku shō ga koku
Fu ka sui sha
<u>Fu</u> <u>shu</u> <u>shō</u> <u>gaku</u> ○

Na man da bu ○
Na man da bu
Na man da bu
Na man da bu
Na man da bu
Na man da bu ○

Gan ni shi ku doku
Byō dō se is-sai
Dō ho'n bo dai shin
Ō jō an rak-koku

○   ○   ○

Shijūhachigan (四十八願)
The Larger Sutra of Immeasurable Life
The Vows of Dharmākara

(11) The Vow of Necessarily Attaining Nirvāna:
"If, when I attain Buddhahood, the humans and devas in my land should not dwell in the stage of the truly settled and necessarily attain nirvāna, may I not attain the perfect enlightenment."

(12) The Vow of Immeasurable Light:
"If, when I attain Buddhahood, my light should be finite, not illuminating even a hundred thousand kotis of nayutas of Buddha-lands, may I not attain the perfect enlightenment."

(13) The Vow of Immeasurable Life:
"If, when I attain Buddhahood, my life should be finite, limited to even a hundred thousand kotis of nayutas of kalpas, may I not attain the perfect enlightenment."

(17) The Vow that All the Buddhas Praise the Name:
"If, when I attain Buddhahood, the countless Buddhas throughout the worlds in the ten quarters should not all glorify and praise my name, may I not attain the perfect enlightenment."

(18) The Vow of Birth through the Nembutsu:
"If, when I attain Buddhahood, the sentient beings of the ten quarters who, with sincere mind and entrusting heart, aspire to be born in my land and say my name even ten times, should not be born there, may I not attain the perfect enlightenment. Excluded are those who commit the five grave offenses and those who slander the right Dharma."

Of the Forty-eight Vows, these five are central to Shinran's teaching. He also emphasizes Vows 19, 20, and 22. For a complete English translation, please see *The Three Pure Land Sutras*, Vol. II, © 2009 Jōdo Shinshū Hongwanji-ha, pp. 20-29.

About the Jūnirai

Jūnirai, or Twelve Verses of Reverence, originated in the Mahāyāna tradition of India during the time of the Pure Land master Nāgārjuna (~150 CE). The verses were later translated into the Chinese text that we chant today.

Like the *Larger Sutra* and the *Amida Sutra*, the text of *Jūnirai* describes the spiritual qualities of Amida and the Pure Land using poetic language: *His practice of truth is steadfast like an elephant's pace, His eyes radiate like pure blue lotus blossoms*, and so forth. The repeating line in verses 2 through 11 is:

故	我	頂	礼	弥	陀	尊
KO	GA	CHŌ	RAI	MI	DA	SON
thus	I	head	bow	"mi"	"da"	noble

GA CHŌ RAI means that I venerate the Buddha with my head touching the ground, the most reverential form of bowing. Here the poet says, "Thus I bow to the ground before Amida, the noble one." This is the perspective of an awakened person who is able to say, "I entrust the totality of my being" to ultimate truth, which is symbolized by Amida and the Pure Land.

When spoken by an awakened person, KO GA CHŌ RAI MI DA SON has the same meaning as "Namo Amida Butsu," that is, "I take refuge in Amida Buddha." However, as foolish beings we lack the perspective through which "I" would cease to be the ego-self. My ego-self can never truly say, "I entrust" or "I take refuge," and so Namo Amida Butsu must be heard as a command to me from ultimate truth: "Take refuge in Amida Buddha!" This is the sense in which we chant KO GA CHŌ RAI MI DA SON.

Jūnirai (十二礼)

Kei shu ten nin sho ku gyō — A mi da sen ryō zo-ku son
Zai hi mi me-u an rak-koku — Mu ryō bus-shi shu i ne-u
2. Kon ji-ki shin jō nyo sen nō — Sha ma ta gyō nyo zō bu
Ryō mo-ku jō nya-ku shō ren ge — Ko ga chō rai mi da son
3. Men zen en jō nyo man gatsu — I kō yu nyo sen ni-chi gatsu
Shō nyo ten ku ku shi ra — Ko ga chō rai mi da son

4.
Kan non chō dai kan chiu jiu
Shu ju meu sō hō shō gon
Nō buku ge dō ma keu man
Ko ga chō rai mi da son

5.
Mu bi mu ku kō shō jō
Shu toku keu ke'n nyo ko kū
Sho sa ri yaku toku ji zai
Ko ga chō rai mi da son

6.
Jip-pō myō mon bo sas-shu
Mu ryō sho ma jō san dan
I sho shu jō gan riki jiu
Ko ga chō rai mi da son

7.
Kon tai hō ken chi shō ke
Zen gon sho jō meu dai za
O hi za jō nyo sen nō
Ko ga chō rai mi da son

8.
Jip-pō sho rai sho bus-shi
Ken gen jin zū shi an raku
Sen gō son gen jō ku gyō
Ko ga chō rai mi da son

9.
Sho u mu jō mu ga tō
Yaku nyo sui ga'n den yō ro
I shu sep-pō mu myō ji
Ko ga chō rai mi da son

10.
Hi son bu-se'n mu aku myō
Yaku mu nyo nin aku dō fu
Shu nin shi shin kyō hi son
Ko ga chō rai mi da son

11.
Hi son mu ryō hō ben kyō
Mu u sho shu aku chi shiki
Ō jō fu tai shi bo dai
Ko ga chō rai mi da son

12.
Ga se'-n hi son ku do-ku ji
Shu zen mu hen nyo kai sui
Sho— gya-ku zen gon sho-u jo—— u sha
E se shu jō—— shō— hi— koku

Na man da bu ○
Na man da bu
Na man da bu
Na man da bu
Na man da bu
Na man da bu ○

Gan ni shi ku doku
Byō dō se is-sai
Dō ho'n bo dai shin
Ō jō an rak-koku

○ ○ ○

Jūnirai (十二礼)
Twelve Verses of Reverence

1.
Devas and people bow to the ground in reverence
Before Amida, the sage, the noble one.
In that marvelous land of peace and bliss,
Countless bodhisattvas surround him.

2.
His golden form shines forth pure, like the king of Mt. Sumeru.
His practice of truth is steadfast, like an elephant's pace.
His eyes radiate like pure blue lotus blossoms.
Thus I bow to the ground before Amida, the noble one.

3.
His face is pure and perfectly shaped like the full moon.
His majestic light shines like a thousand suns and moons.
His voice is like a heavenly drum or like a heavenly bird.
Thus I bow to the ground before Amida, the noble one.

4.
Bodhisattva Kannon wears upon his crown
The image of Amida adorned with many precious jewels
To subdue non-Buddhist views and the arrogance of maras.
Thus I bow to the ground before Amida, the noble one.

5.
His virtues are incomparable, vast, and pure,
Clearly extending like vast open space.
His acts freely benefit all beings.
Thus I bow to the ground before Amida, the noble one.

6.
Bodhisattvas renowned throughout the ten quarters
And even countless maras always venerate him.
The power of Amida's vow is for the benefit of all beings.
Thus I bow to the ground before Amida, the noble one.

7.
Lotus flowers bloom in the golden treasure-pond.
Meritorious acts establish a wondrous throne,
And upon it sits Amida, like the king of Mt. Sumeru.
Thus I bow to the ground before Amida, the noble one.

8.
From the ten quarters bodhisattvas come.
Revealing wondrous powers, they realize peace and bliss.
Honoring his face, they offer eternal homage.
Thus I bow to the ground before Amida, the noble one.

9.
All things are impermanent and without self,
Like the moon on water, lightning, shadow, or dew.
Multitudes benefit from the Dharma that is beyond words.
Thus I bow to the ground before Amida, the noble one.

10.
In the Buddha's temple there are no evil names,
Nor is there discrimination or fearful evil paths.
Every person having a sincere mind reveres the Buddha.
Thus I bow to the ground before Amida, the noble one.

11.
The Buddha's countless skillful means
Put an end to renewed existence and to evil understandings.
To be born is to attain non-retrogression toward Buddhahood.
Thus I bow to the ground before Amida, the noble one.

12.
Thus have I praised the virtues of Amida.
His meritorious acts are as boundless as the waters of the sea.
Upon receiving these pure and good qualities,
May all beings be born into his land.

From the *Shinshū Seiten*, Buddhist Churches of America, 1978, [translation revised by OCBC].

Jūnirai (十二礼)

○○

けいしゅ　てん　にん　しょ　く　ぎょう
稽首天人所恭敬

あ　み　だ　せん　りょう　ぞく　そん
阿弥陀仙両足尊

ざい　ひ　み　めう　あん　らっ　こく
在彼微妙安楽国

む　りょう　ぶっ　し　しゅ　い　ねう
無量仏子衆囲繞

こん　じき　しん　じょう　にょ　せん　のう
金色身浄如山王

しゃ　ま　た　ぎょう　にょ　ぞう　ぶ
奢摩他行如象歩

りょう　もく　じょう　にょく　しょう　れん　げ
両目浄若青蓮華

こ　が　ちょう　らい　み　だ　そん
故我頂礼弥陀尊

めん　ぜん　えん　じょう　にょ　まん　がつ
面善円浄如満月

い　こう　ゆ　にょ　せん　にち　がつ
威光猶如千日月

しょう　にょ　てん　く　く　し　ら
声如天鼓倶翅羅

こ　が　ちょう　らい　み　だ　そん
故我頂礼弥陀尊

かん　のん　ちょう　だい　かん　ちう　じう
観音頂戴冠中住

しゅ　じゅ　めう　そう　ほう　しょう　ごん
種種妙相宝荘厳

のう　ぶく　げ　どう　ま　けう　まん
能伏外道魔憍慢

こ　が　ちょう　らい　み　だ　そん
故我頂礼弥陀尊

む　び　む　く　こう　しょう　じょう
無比無垢広清浄

しゅ　とく　けう　けつ　にょ　こ　く
衆徳皎潔如虚空

しょ　さ　り　やく　とく　じ　ざい
所作利益得自在

こ　が　ちょう　らい　み　だ　そん
故我頂礼弥陀尊

じっ　ぽう　みょう　もん　ぼ　さっ　しゅ
十方名聞菩薩衆

む　りょう　しょ　ま　じょう　さん　だん
無量諸摩常讃歎

い　しょ　しゅ　じょう　がん　りき　じゅう
為諸衆生願力住

こ　が　ちょう　らい　み　だ　そん
故我頂礼弥陀尊

こん　たい　ほう　けん　ち　しょう　け
金底宝間池生華

ぜん　ごん　しょ　じょう　めう　だい　ざ
善根所成妙台座

お　ひ　ざ　じょう　にょ　せん　のう
於彼座上如山王

こ　が　ちょう　らい　み　だ　そん
故我頂礼弥陀尊

じっ　ぽう　しょ　らい　しょ　ぶっ　し
十方所来諸仏子

けん　げん　じん　ずう　し　あん　らく
顕現神通至安楽

せん　ごう　そん　げん　じょう　く　ぎょう
瞻仰尊顔常恭敬

こ　が　ちょう　らい　み　だ　そん
故我頂礼弥陀尊

諸(しょ)有(う)無(む)常(じょう)無(む)我(が)等(とう)
亦(やく)如(にょ)水(すい)月(がつ)電(でん)影(よう)露(ろ)
為(い)衆(しゅ)説(せっ)法(ぽう)無(む)名(みょう)字(じ)
故(こ)我(が)頂(ちょう)礼(らい)弥(み)陀(だ)尊(そん)

彼(ひ)尊(そん)仏(ぶっ)刹(せつ)無(む)悪(あく)名(みょう)
亦(やく)無(む)女(にょ)人(にん)悪(あく)道(どう)怖(ぶ)
衆(しゅ)人(にん)至(し)心(しん)敬(きょう)彼(ひ)尊(そん)
故(こ)我(が)頂(ちょう)礼(らい)弥(み)陀(だ)尊(そん)

彼(ひ)尊(そん)無(む)量(りょう)方(ほう)便(べん)境(きょう)
無(む)有(う)諸(しょ)趣(しゅ)悪(あく)知(ち)識(しき)
往(おう)生(じょう)不(ふ)退(たい)至(し)菩(ぼ)提(だい)
故(こ)我(が)頂(ちょう)礼(らい)弥(み)陀(だ)尊(そん)

我(が)説(せつ)彼(ひ)尊(そん)功(く)徳(どく)事(じ)
衆(しゅ)善(ぜん)無(む)辺(へん)如(にょ)海(かい)水(すい)
所(しょ)獲(ぎゃく)善(ぜん)根(ごん)清(しょう)浄(じょう)者(しゃ)
回(え)施(せ)衆(しゅ)生(じょう)生(しょう)彼(ひ)国(こく)。

南(な)无(ー)阿(まー)弥(ん)陀(だー)仏(ぶー)。
南无阿弥陀仏
南无阿弥陀仏
南无阿弥陀仏
南无阿弥陀仏
南无阿弥陀仏。

願(がん)以(に)此(し)功(く)徳(どく)
平(びょう)等(どう)施(せ)一(いち)切(さい)
同(どう)発(ほつ)菩(ぼ)提(だい)心(しん)
往(おう)生(じょう)安(あん)楽(らっ)国(こく)。○○

About the Amida Sutra

Along with the *Larger Sutra of Immeasurable Life* and the *Contemplation Sutra*, the *Amida Sutra* is one of the central texts of Pure Land Buddhism in China and Japan. Because the *Amida Sutra* is relatively brief, it is often chanted in its entirety.

In the sutra, Śākyamuni addresses Śāriputra and the other disciples, describing in poetic language the Land of Perfect Bliss where Amida Buddha resides, and urging that "all sentient beings who hear this teaching should aspire for birth in that Land." Śākyamuni then proclaims the fulfillment of this aspiration:

"Those persons who have already aspired, now aspire, or will aspire to be born in the Land of Amida Buddha, all dwell in the stage of non-retrogression for attaining the supreme, perfect enlightenment. They have already been born, are now being born, or will be born in that Land."

Śākyamuni concludes by stating the reason he gave this teaching:

"In the midst of this evil world of the five defilements, I have accomplished this difficult task. I have attained the supreme, perfect enlightenment, and for the sake of all beings of the world, I am expounding this teaching which is difficult to accept. This is an extremely difficult task."

For an English translation of the *Amida Sutra* with explanatory material, please refer to *The Three Pure Land Sutras*, Vol. I, © 2003 Jōdo Shinshū Hongwanji-ha.

Amida Sutra (阿弥陀経)

○ ○

Bus-setsu a mi da kyō
Nyo ze ga mon
Ichi ji butsu zai
Sha e koku
Gi ju kik-ko doku on
Yo dai bi ku shu
Sen ni hyaku go jū nin ku
Kai ze dai a ra kan
Shu sho chi shiki
Chō rō sha ri hotsu
Ma ka mok-ken ren
Ma ka ka shō
Ma ka ka sen nen
Ma ka ku chi ra
Ri ha ta
Shu ri han da ga
Nan da
A nan da
Ra go ra
Kyō bon ha dai
Bin zu ru ha ra da
Ka ru da i
Ma ka kō hin na
Ha ku ra
A nu ru da
Nyo ze tō
Sho dai de shi
Byō sho bo satsu ma ka satsu
Mon ju shi ri hō ō ji
A it-ta bo satsu
Ken da ka dai bo satsu
Jō shō jin bo satsu
Yo nyo ze tō
Sho dai bo satsu
Gyū shaku dai kan in tō
Mu ryō sho ten
Dai shu ku

Ni ji butsu gō
Chō rō sha ri hotsu
Ju ze sai hō
Ka jū man-noku butsu do
U se kai
Myō watsu goku raku
Go do u butsu
Gō a mi da
Kon gen zai sep-pō
—
Sha ri hotsu
Hi do ga ko
Myō i goku raku
Go koku shu jō
Mu u shu ku
Tan ju sho raku
Ko myō goku raku
—
U sha ri hotsu
Goku rak-koku do
Shichi jū ran jun
Shichi jū ra mō
Shichi jū gō ju
Kai ze shi hō
Shu sō i nyō
Ze ko hi koku
Myō watsu goku raku
—
U sha ri hotsu
Goku rak-koku do
U ship-pō chi
Hak-ku doku sui
Jū man go chū
Chi tai jun-ni
Kon sha fu ji
Shi hen kai dō
Kon gon ru ri

Ha ri gō jō
Jō u rō kaku
Yaku i kon gon ru ri
Ha ri sha ko
Shaku shu me nō
Ni gon jiki shi
Chi chū ren ge
Dai nyo sha rin
Shō shiki shō kō
Ō shiki ō kō
Shaku shiki shak-kō
Byaku shiki byak-kō
Mi myō kō ketsu
Sha ri hotsu
Goku rak-koku do
Jō ju nyo ze
Ku doku shō gon
—
U sha ri hotsu
Hi buk-koku do
Jō sa ten gaku
Ō gon i ji
Chū ya roku ji
Ni u man da ra ke
Go koku shu jō
Jō i shō tan
Kaku i e koku
Jō shu myō ke
Ku yō ta hō
Jū man-noku butsu
Soku i jiki ji
Gen tō hon goku
Bon jiki kyō gyō
Sha ri hotsu
Goku rak-koku do
Jō ju nyo ze
Ku doku shō gon
—
Bu shi sha ri hotsu
Hi koku jō u

Shu ju ki myō
Zas-shiki shi chō
Byak-kō ku jaku
Ō mu sha ri
Ka ryō bin ga
Gu myō shi chō
Ze sho shu chō
Chū ya roku ji
Sui wa ge on
Go on en chō
Go kon go riki
Shichi bo dai bun
Has-shō dō bun
Nyo ze tō hō
Go do shu jō
Mon ze on-ni
Kai shitsu nen butsu
Nen pō nen sō
Sha ri hotsu
Nyo motsu i shi chō
Jitsu ze zai hō sho shō
Sho i sha ga
Hi buk-koku do
Mu sam-maku shu
Sha ri hotsu
Go buk-koku do
Shō mu sam-maku dō shi myō
Ga kyō u jitsu
Ze sho shu chō
Kai ze a mi da butsu
Yoku ryō hō on sen ru
Hen ge sho sa
Sha ri hotsu
Hi buk-koku do
Mi fu sui dō
Sho hō gō ju
Gyū hō ra mō
Sui mi myō on
Hi nyo hyaku sen ju gaku
Dō ji ku sa

Mon ze on sha
Kai ji nen jō
Nen butsu nen pō
Nen sō shi shin
Sha ri hotsu
Go buk-koku do
<u>Jō ju nyo ze</u>
<u>Kudoku shō gon</u>
     o o o

Sha ri hotsu
O nyo i un ga
Hi butsu ga ko
Gō a mi da
Sha ri hotsu
Hi butsu kō myō mu ryō
Shō jip-pō koku
Mu sho shō ge
Ze ko gō i a mi da
U sha ri hotsu
Hi butsu ju myō
Gyū go nin min
Mu ryō mu hen
A sō gi kō
Ko myō a mi da
Sha ri hotsu
A mi da butsu
Jō butsu i rai
O kon jik-kō
U sha ri hotsu
Hi butsu u mu ryō mu hen
Shō mon de shi
Kai a ra kan
Hi ze san ju
Shi sho nō chi
Sho bo sas-shu
Yaku bu nyo ze
Sha ri hotsu
Hi buk-koku do
Jō ju nyo ze
Ku doku shō gon

U sha ri hotsu
Goku rak-koku do
Shu jō shō ja
Kai ze a bi bac-chi
Go chū ta u
Is-shō fu sho
Go shu jin ta
Hi ze san ju
Sho nō chi shi
Tan ka i mu ryō mu hen
A sō gi kō setsu
Sha ri hotsu
Shu jō mon sha
Ō tō hotsu gan
Gan shō hi koku
Sho i sha ga
Toku yo nyo ze
Sho jō zen nin
Ku e is-sho
Sha ri hotsu
Fu ka i shō zen gon
Fuku toku in-nen
Toku shō hi koku
—
Sha ri hotsu
Nyaku u zen nan shi
Zen nyo nin
Mon setsu a mi da butsu
Shū ji myō gō
Nyaku ichi nichi
Nyaku ni nichi
Nyaku san nichi
Nyaku shi nichi
Nyaku go nichi
Nyaku roku nichi
Nyaku shichi nichi
Is-shin fu ran
Go nin rin myō ju ji
A mi da butsu
Yo sho shō ju

Gen zai go zen
Ze nin ju ji
Shin pu ten dō
Soku toku ō jō
A mi da butsu
Goku rak-koku do
Sha ri hotsu
Ga ken ze ri
Ko ses-shi gon
Nyaku u shu jō
Mon ze ses-sha
Ō tō hotsu gan
Shō hi koku do
—
Sha ri hotsu
Nyo ga kon ja
San dan a mi da butsu
Fu ka shi gi ku doku
Tō bō yaku u
A shuku bi butsu
Shu mi sō butsu
Dai shu mi butsu
Shu mi kō butsu
Myō on butsu
Nyo ze tō
Gō ga sha shu sho butsu
Kaku o go koku
Sui kō jō zes-sō
Hen pu san zen
Dai sen se kai
Setsu jō jitsu gon
Nyo tō shu jō
Tō shin ze shō san
Fu ka shi gi ku doku
Is-sai sho butsu
Sho go nen gyō
—
Sha ri hotsu
Nan bō se kai
U nichi gat-tō butsu

Myō mon kō butsu
Dai en ken butsu
Shu mi tō butsu
Mu ryō shō jin butsu
Nyo ze tō
Gō ga sha shu sho butsu
Kaku o go koku
Sui kō jō zes-sō
Hen pu san zen
Dai sen se kai
Setsu jō jitsu gon
Nyo tō shu jō
Tō shin ze shō san
Fu ka shi gi ku doku
Is-sai sho butsu
Sho go nen gyō
—
Sha ri hotsu
Sai hō se kai
U mu ryō ju butsu
Mu ryō sō butsu
Mu ryō dō butsu
Dai kō butsu
Dai myō butsu
Hō sō butsu
Jō kō butsu
Nyo ze tō
Gō ga sha shu sho butsu
Kaku o go koku
Sui kō jō zes-sō
Hen pu san zen
Dai sen se kai
Setsu jō jitsu gon
Nyo tō shu jō
Tō shin ze shō san
Fu ka shi gi ku doku
Is-sai sho butsu
Sho go nen gyō
—
Sha ri hotsu

Hop-pō se kai
U en ken butsu
Sai shō on butsu
Nan sho butsu
Nis-shō butsu
Mō myō butsu
Nyo ze tō
Gō ga sha shu sho butsu
Kaku o go koku
Sui kō jō zes-sō
Hen pu san zen
Dai sen se kai
Setsu jō jitsu gon
Nyo tō shu jō
Tō shin ze shō san
Fu ka shi gi ku doku
Is-sai sho butsu
Sho go nen gyō
—

Sha ri hotsu
Ge hō se kai
U shi shi butsu
Myō mon butsu
Myō kō butsu
Datsu ma butsu
Hō dō butsu
Ji hō butsu
Nyo ze tō
Gō ga sha shu sho butsu
Kaku o go koku
Sui kō jō zes-sō
Hen pu san zen
Dai sen se kai
Setsu jō jitsu gon
Nyo tō shu jō
Tō shin ze shō san
Fu ka shi gi ku doku
Is-sai sho butsu
Sho go nen gyō
—

Sha ri hotsu
Jō hō se kai
U bon-non butsu
Shuku ō butsu
Kō jō butsu
Kō kō butsu
Dai en ken butsu
Zas-shiki hō ke gon shin butsu
Sha ra ju ō butsu
Hō ke toku butsu
Ken is-sai gi butsu
Nyo shu mi sen butsu
Nyo ze tō
Gō ga sha shu sho butsu
Kaku o go koku
Sui kō jō zes-sō
Hen pu san zen
Dai sen se kai
Setsu jō jitsu gon
Nyo tō shu jō
Tō shin ze shō san
Fu ka shi gi ku doku
Is-sai sho butsu
Sho go nen gyō
—

Sha ri hotsu
O nyo i un ga
Ga ko myō i
Is-sai sho butsu
Sho go nen gyō
Sha ri hotsu
Nyaku u zen nan shi
Zen nyo nin
Mon ze sho bus-sho setsu myō
Gyū kyō myō sha
Ze sho zen nan shi
Zen nyo nin
Kai i is-sai sho butsu
Gu sho go nen
Kai toku fu tai ten

Amida Sutra

O a noku ta ra
Sam-myaku san bo dai
Ze ko sha ri hotsu
Nyo tō kai tō
Shin ju ga go
Gis-sho bus-sho setsu
Sha ri hotsu
Nyaku u nin
I hotsu gan
Kon potsu gan
Tō hotsu gan
Yoku shō a mi da buk-koku sha
Ze sho nin tō
Kai toku fu tai ten
O a noku ta ra
Sam-myaku san bo dai
O hi koku do
Nyaku i shō
Nyaku kon jō
Nyaku tō shō
Ze ko sha ri hotsu
Sho zen nan shi
Zen nyo nin
Nyaku u shin ja
Ō tō hotsu gan
Shō hi koku do
—
Sha ri hotsu
Nyo ga kon ja
Shō san sho butsu
Fu ka shi gi ku doku
Hi sho but-tō
Yaku shō setsu ga
Fu ka shi gi ku doku
Ni sa ze gon
Shaka muni butsu
Nō i jin nan
Ke u shi ji
Nō o sha ba koku do
Go joku aku se

Kō joku ken joku
Bon nō joku
Shu jō joku
Myō joku chū
Toku a noku ta ra
Sam-myaku san bo dai
I sho shu jō
Setsu ze is-sai se ken
Nan shin shi hō
Sha ri hotsu
Tō chi ga o
Go joku aku se
Gyō shi nan ji
Toku a noku ta ra
Sam-myaku san bo dai
I is-sai se ken
Ses-shi nan shin shi hō
Ze i jin nan
—
Bus-se-shi kyō i
Sha ri hotsu
Gis-sho bi ku
Is-sai se ken
Ten nin ashu ra tō
Mon bus-shosetsu
Kan gi shin ju
Sarai niko
Bus-setsu a mi da kyō ○
—
Na man da bu ○
Na man da bu
Na man da bu
Na man da bu
Na man da bu
Na man da bu ○
—
Gan ni shi ku doku
Byō dō se is-sai
Dō ho'n bo dai shin
Ō jō an rak-koku ○ ○ ○

About the Shōshinge

The full title of Shinran's poem is

正	信	念	仏	偈
SHŌ	SHIN	NEN	BUTSU	GE

or "Verses on True Shinjin and Nembutsu." It contains 30 verses with seven Chinese characters per line, beginning with:

帰	命	無	量	寿	如	来
KI	MYŌ	MU	RYŌ	JU	NYO	RAI
南	无	不	可	思	議	光
NA	MO	FU	KA	SHI	GI	KŌ

Verses 1 through 11 are Shinran's unique interpretation of the *Larger Sutra*. Verses 12 through 30 honor Śākyamuni and the seven Pure Land masters who transmitted this teaching to Shinran:

Śākyamuni (*Shaka*)	India	~450 BCE
Nāgārjuna (*Ryūju*)	India	~150 CE
Vasubandhu (*Tenjin*)	India	~350
T'an-luan (*Donran*)	China	476-542
Tao-ch'o (*Dōshaku*)	China	562-645
Shan-tao (*Zendō*)	China	613-681
Eshin-in (*Genshin*)	Japan	942-1017
Hōnen (*Genkū*)	Japan	1133-1212
Shinran (*Gutoku*)	Japan	1173-1262

We chant *Shōshinge* in the original language using traditional melodies. In the Buddhist Churches of America, the three chanting styles most often used are called *Sōfu*, *Gyōfu*, and *Jūnirai*. After *Shōshinge* we chant the *Nembutsu Wasan*, a group of six of Shinran's Japanese language poems accompanied by nembutsu recitation. Each *wasan* verse begins with a leader line chanted by the minister.

Shōshinge (正信偈)
Gyō-fu (行譜)

Ki myo-u mu ryo-u ju nyo ra-i Na mo fu ka shi gi kō

Hō zō bo sa-tsu in ni ji Zai se ji zai ō bus-sho

2.
To ken sho butsu jō do in
Koku do nin den shi zen maku
Kon ryū mu jō shu shō gan
Chō hotsu <u>ke</u>-u <u>dai</u> gu zei

3.
Go kō shi yui shi shō ju
Jū sei myō shō mon jip-pō
Fu hō mu ryō mu hen kō
Mu ge mu tai kō en nō

4.
Shō jō kan gi chi e kō
Fu dan nan ji mu shō kō
Chō nichi gakkō shō jin setsu
Is-sai gunjō mu kō shō

5.
Hon gan myō gō shō jō gō
Shi shin shin gyō gan ni in
Jō tō gaku shō dai ne han
His-shi metsu do gan jō ju

6.
Nyo rai <u>sho</u>-i kō shus-se
Yui setsu mi da hon gan kai
Go joku aku ji gun jō kai
Ō shin nyo rai nyo jitsu gon

7.
Nō hotsu ichi nen ki ai shin
Fu dan bon nō toku ne han
Bon jō gyaku hō sai e nyū
Nyo shu shi nyū kai ichi mi

8.
Ses-shu shin kō jō shō go
I nō sui ha mu myō an
Ton nai shin zō shi un mu
<u>Jō</u>-fu shin jitsu shin jin ten

9.
Hi nyo nik-kō fu un mu
Un mu shi ge <u>myō</u>-mu an
Gyaku shin ken kyō dai kyō ki
Soku ō chō zetsu go aku shu

10.
Is-sai zen maku bon bu nin
Mon shin nyo rai gu zei gan
Butsu gon kō dai shō ge sha
Ze nin <u>myō</u> fun da ri ke—

11.
—mi da butsu hon gan nen butsu
Ja ken kyō man aku shu jō
Shin gyō ju ji jin ni nan
Nan chū shi nan mu ka shi

Shōshinge Gyōfu

16.
Tenjin bo satsu zō ron setsu
Ki myō mu ge kō nyo rai
E shu ta ra ken shin jitsu
Kō sen ō chō dai sei gan

17.
K<u>ō</u>-yu hon gan riki e kō
I do gun jō shō is-shin
Ki nyū ku doku dai hō kai
Hitsu gyaku nyū dai e shu shu

18.
Toku shi ren ge zō se kai
Soku shō shin nyo hos-shō jin
Yu bon nō rin gen jin zū
Nyū shō ji on ji ō ge

19.
Hon shi *Donran* ryō ten shi
Jō kō ran sho bo satsu rai
San zō ru shi ju jō kyō
Bon jō sen gyō ki raku hō

20.
Tenjin bo satsu ron chū ge
Hō do in ga ken sei gan
Ō gen ne kō yu ta riki
Shō jō shi in yui shin jin

21.
Waku zen bon bu shin jin potsu
<u>Shō</u>-chi <u>shō</u>-ji soku ne han
His-shi mu ryō kō myō do
<u>Sho</u>-u shu jō kai fu ke

22.
Dōshaku kes-shō dō nan shō
Yui myō jō do ka tsū nyū
Man zen ji riki hen gon shu
En man toku gō kan sen shō

23.
<u>San</u>-pu san shin ke on gon
Zo matsu hō metsu <u>dō</u>-hi in
Is-shō zō aku chi gu zei
Shi <u>an</u> <u>nyō</u> <u>gai</u> <u>shō</u> <u>myō</u> ka

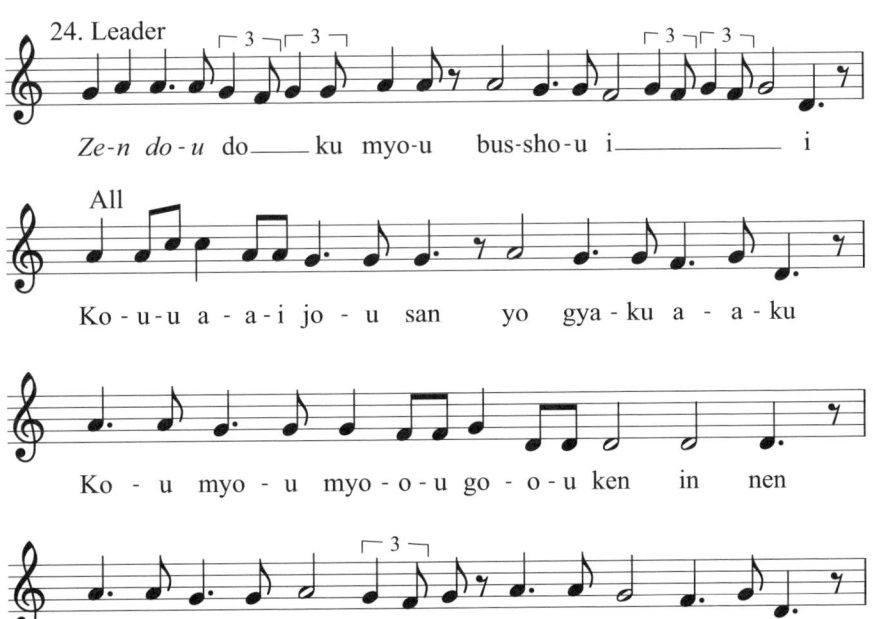

24. Leader: Ze-n do-u do——ku myo-u bus-sho-u i———— i

All: Ko-u-u a-a-i jo-u san yo gya-ku a-a-ku

Ko-u myo-u myo-o-u go-o-u ken in nen

Ka-i ni-u hon ga-a-n da-i chi ka-a-i

Shōshinge (正信偈)
Sō-fu (草譜)

Ki myo - u mu ryo - u ju nyo ra - i   Na mo fu ka shi gi kō

Hō zō bo sa-tsu in ni ji   Zai se ji zai ō bus-sho

2.
To ken sho bu-tsu jō do in   Ko-ku do nin den shi zen maku

Kon ryū mu jō shu shō gan   Chō ho-tsu ke u dai gu zei

3.
Go kō shi yui shi shō ju
Jū sei myō shō mon jip-pō
Fu hō mu ryō mu hen kō
Mu ge mu tai kō en nō

4.
Shō jō kan gi chi e kō
Fu dan nan ji mu shō kō
Chō nichi gakkō shō jin setsu
Is-sai gunjō mu kō shō

5.
Hon gan myō gō shō jō gō
Shi shin shin gyō gan ni in
Jō tō gaku shō dai ne han
His-shi metsu do gan jō ju

6.
Nyo rai sho-i kō shus-se
Yui setsu mi da hon gan kai
Go joku aku ji gun jō kai
Ō shin nyo rai nyo jitsu gon

7.
Nō hotsu ichi nen ki ai shin
Fu dan bon nō toku ne han
Bon jō gyaku hō sai e nyū
Nyo shu shi nyū kai ichi mi

8.
Ses-shu shin kō jō shō go
I nō sui ha mu myō an
Ton nai shin zō shi un mu
Jō-fu shin jitsu shin jin ten

9.
Hi nyo nik-kō fu un mu
Un mu shi ge _myō_-mu an
Gyaku shin ken kyō dai kyō ki
Soku ō chō zetsu go aku shu

10.
Is-sai zen maku bon bu nin
Mon shin nyo rai gu zei gan
Butsu gon kō dai shō ge sha
Ze nin _myō_ fun da ri ke—

11.
—mi da butsu hon gan nen butsu
Ja ken kyō man aku shu jō
Shin gyō ju ji jin ni nan
Nan chū shi nan mu ka shi

12.
In do sai ten shi ron ge
Chū ka jichi iki shi kō sō
Ken dai shō kō se shō i
Myō nyo rai hon zei ō ki

13.
Shaka nyo rai ryō ga sen
I _shu_ _gō_ _myō_ nan ten jiku
Ryūju _dai_-ji shut-to se
Shitsu nō zai ha u mu ken

14.
Sen zetsu dai jō mu jō hō
Shō kan gi ji shō an raku
Ken ji nan gyō roku ro ku
Shin gyō i gyō shi dō raku

15.
Oku nen mi da butsu hon gan
Ji _nen_ _soku_ _ji_ nyū hitsu jō
Yui nō jō shō nyo rai gō
Ō hō _dai_-hi gu zei on

16.
Tenjin bo satsu zō ron setsu
Ki myō mu ge kō nyo rai
E shu ta ra ken shin jitsu
Kō sen ō chō dai sei gan

17.
Kō-yu hon gan riki e kō
I do gun jō shō is-shin
Ki nyū ku doku dai hō kai
Hitsu gyaku nyū dai e shu shu

18.
Toku shi ren ge zō se kai
Soku shō shin nyo hos-shō jin
Yu bon nō rin gen jin zū
Nyū shō ji on ji ō ge

19.
Hon shi *Donran* ryō ten shi
Jō kō ran sho bo satsu rai
San zō ru shi ju jō kyō
Bon jō sen gyō ki raku hō

20.
Tenjin bo satsu ron chū ge
Hō do in ga ken sei gan
Ō gen ne kō yu ta riki
Shō jō shi in yui shin jin

21.
Waku zen bon bu shin jin potsu
Shō-chi shō-ji soku ne han
His-shi mu ryō kō myō do
Sho-u shu jō kai fu ke

22.
Dōshaku kes-shō dō nan shō
Yui myō jō do ka tsū nyū
Man zen ji riki hen gon shu
En man toku gō kan sen shō

Shōshinge (正信偈)
Jūnirai (十二礼)

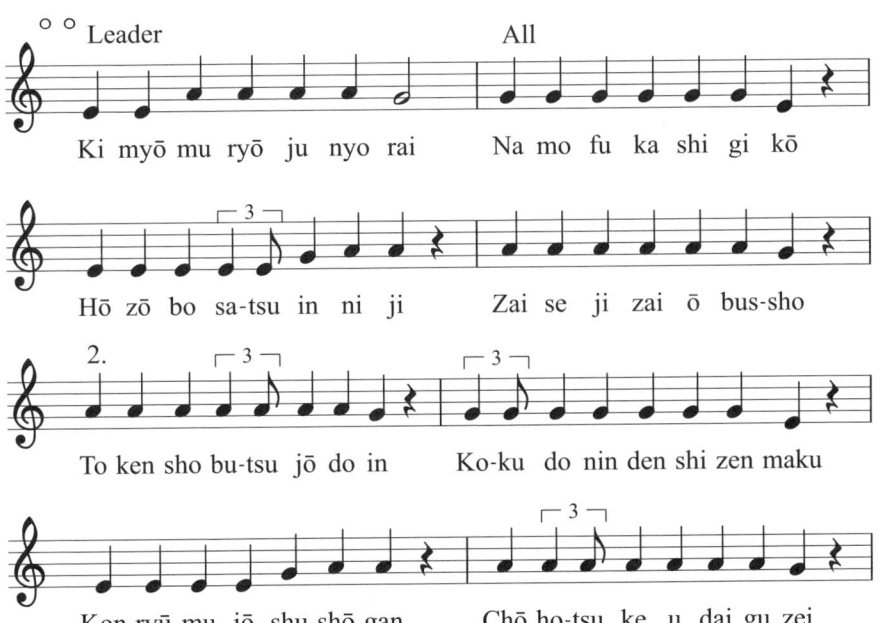

3.
Go kō shi yui shi shō ju
Jū sei myō shō mon jip-pō
Fu hō mu ryō mu hen kō
Mu ge mu tai kō en nō

4.
Shō jō kan gi chi e kō
Fu dan nan ji mu shō kō
Chō nichi gakkō shō jin setsu
Is-sai gunjō mu kō shō

5.
Hon gan myō gō shō jō gō
Shi shin shin gyō gan ni in
Jō tō gaku shō dai ne han
His-shi metsu do gan jō ju

6.
Nyo rai sho i kō shus-se
Yui setsu mi da hon gan kai
Go joku aku ji gun jō kai
Ō shin nyo rai nyo jitsu gon

7.
Nō hotsu ichi nen ki ai shin
Fu dan bon nō toku ne han
Bon jō gyaku hō sai e nyū
Nyo shu shi nyū kai ichi mi

8.
Ses-shu shin kō jō shō go
I nō sui ha mu myō an
Ton nai shin zō shi un mu
Jō fu shin jitsu shin jin ten

9.
Hi nyo nik-kō fu un mu
Un mu shi ge myō mu an
Gyaku shin ken kyō dai kyō ki
Soku ō chō zetsu go aku shu

10.
Is-sai zen maku bon bu nin
Mon shin nyo rai gu zei gan
Butsu gon kō dai shō ge sha
Ze nin myō fun da ri ke

11.
Mi da butsu hon gan nen butsu
Ja ken kyō man aku shu jō
Shin gyō ju ji jin ni nan
Nan chū shi nan mu ka shi

12.
In do sai ten shi ron ge
Chū ka jichi iki shi kō sō
Ken dai shō kō se shō i
Myō nyo rai hon zei ō ki

13.
Shaka nyo rai ryō ga sen
I shu gō myō nan ten jiku
Ryūju dai ji shut-to se
Shitsu nō zai ha u mu ken

14.
Sen zetsu dai jō mu jō hō
Shō kan gi ji shō an raku
Ken ji nan gyō roku ro ku
Shin gyō i gyō shi dō raku

15.
Oku nen mi da butsu hon gan
Ji nen soku ji nyū hitsu jō
Yui nō jō shō nyo rai gō
Ō hō dai hi gu zei on

16.
Tenjin bo satsu zō ron setsu
Ki myō mu ge kō nyo rai
E shu ta ra ken shin jitsu
Kō sen ō chō dai sei gan

17.
Kō yu hon gan riki e kō
I do gun jō shō is-shin
Ki nyū ku doku dai hō kai
Hitsu gyaku nyū dai e shu shu

18.
Toku shi ren ge zō se kai
Soku shō shin nyo hos-shō jin
Yu bon nō rin gen jin zū
Nyū shō ji on ji ō ge

19.
Hon shi *Donran* ryō ten shi
Jō kō ran sho bo satsu rai
San zō ru shi ju jō kyō
Bon jō sen gyō ki raku hō

20.
Tenjin bo satsu ron chū ge
Hō do in ga ken sei gan
Ō gen ne kō yu ta riki
Shō jō shi in yui shin jin

21.
Waku zen bon bu shin jin potsu
Shō chi shō ji soku ne han
His-shi mu ryō kō myō do
Sho u shu jō kai fu ke

22.
Dōshaku kes-shō dō nan shō
Yui myō jō do ka tsū nyū
Man zen ji riki hen gon shu
En man toku gō kan sen shō

23.
San pu san shin ke on gon
Zō matsu hō metsu dō hi in
Is-shō zō aku chi gu zei
Shi an nyō gai shō myō ka

24.
Zendō doku myō bus-shō i
Kō ai jō san yo gyaku aku
Kō myō myō gō ken in nen
Kai nyū hon gan dai chi kai

25.
Gyō ja shō ju kon gō shin
Kyō ki ichi nen sō ō go
Yo i dai tō gyaku san nin
Soku shō hos-shō shi jō raku

26.
Genshin kō kai ichi dai kyō
Hen ki an nyō kan is-sai
Sen zō shū shin han sen jin
Hō ke ni do shō ben ryū

27.
Goku jū aku nin yui shō butsu
Ga yaku zai hi ses-shu chū
Bon nō shō gen sui fu ken
Dai hi mu ken jō shō ga

28.
Hon shi *Genkū* myō buk-kyō
Ren min zen maku bon bu nin
Shin shū kyō shō kō hen shū
Sen jaku hon gan gu aku se

29.
Gen rai shō ji rin den ge
Ket-chi gi jō i sho shi
So-ku nyū ja-ku jō mu i raku
Hit-chi shin jin i nō nyū

30.
Gu kyō dai ji shū shi tō
Jō sai mu hen go-ku jo-ku aku
Do-u zo-ku ji shu gu do-u shin
Yu-i ka shin shi ko-u so-u setsu

Nembutsu Wasan (念仏和讃)
Verses in Praise of Amida Buddha

Nembutsu Wasan

Nembutsu Wasan

Nembutsu Wasan

Nembutsu Wasan

Nembutsu Wasan in English
Verses in Praise of Amida Buddha

1.
Amida has passed through ten kalpas now
Since realizing Buddhahood;
Dharma-body's wheel of light is without bound,
Shining on the blind and ignorant of the world.

2.
The light of wisdom exceeds all measure,
And every finite living being
Receives this illumination that is like the dawn,
So take refuge in Amida, the true and real light.

3.
The liberating wheel of light is without bound;
Each person it touches, it is taught,
Is freed from attachments to being and non-being,
So take refuge in Amida, the enlightenment of non-discrimination.

4.
The cloud of light is unhindered, like open sky;
There is nothing that impedes it.
Every being is nurtured by this light,
So take refuge in Amida, the one beyond conception.

5.
The light of purity is without compare.
When a person encounters this light,
All bonds of karma fall away;
So take refuge in Amida, the ultimate shelter.

6.
The Buddha's light is supreme in radiance;
Thus Amida is called, "Buddha, Lord of Blazing Light."
It dispels the darkness of the three courses of affliction,
So take refuge in Amida, the great one worthy of offerings.

From *The Collected Works of Shinran*, Vol. 1, © 1997 Jōdo Shinshū Hongwanji-ha, pp. 325-326.

Chanting

Shōshinge in English Prose (正信偈)
Verses on True Shinjin and Nembutsu

1.
In the Tathāgata of Immeasurable Life, take refuge!
In the Light that surpasses all thoughts or ideas, take refuge!
Dharmākara, while on the bodhisattva path
And under the guidance of the Buddha, Spiritual King Who Lived Freely in Samsara,

2.
Observed with deep concentration the origins of the Buddhas' pure lands
And everything about those lands, including the positive and the negative, the human and heavenly.
Then Dharmākara's unsurpassed, excellent Aspirations—
The all-encompassing Vows of universal deliverance—came forth.

3.
After timeless, profound contemplation on how to realize his Aspirations,
He vowed that his names would be heard everywhere:
Light Immeasurable, Light Unlimited,
Light Unobstructed, Light Incomparable, Light of Utmost Brilliance,

4.
Light of Purity, Light of Joyfulness, Light of Wisdom,
Light Unceasing, Light Inconceivable, Light Beyond Description,
Light Surpassing the Sun and Moon. This Light illuminates countless worlds
And shines on all sentient beings.

5.
The Vow of Amida Buddha's Name expresses the right practice that assures our truly settled state [of eventual liberation]. [17th Vow]
The Vow of Sincere Mind and Joyful Entrusting expresses the cause of our attaining Buddhahood. [18th Vow]
Realizing the highest bodhisattva stage—the equal of perfect enlightenment—
Fulfills the Vow of Definitely Assured Liberation. [11th Vow]

6.
Śākyamuni Buddha appeared in this world
Solely to share the ocean-like Innermost Aspiration of Amida.
We multitudes of beings living in a time of five defilements
Should entrust ourselves to the truth of the words of the Buddha.

7.
When one thought-moment of joy and gratitude awakens in us,
We shall experience liberation without severing blind passions.
When ignorant and wise people, including grave offenders and slanderers of the
    Dharma, are in the grasp of the Vow,
They are like the waters that, on entering the ocean, become one in taste with it.

8.
The light of all-embracing Compassion shines on us and protects us always,
Breaking through the darkness of ignorance;
Even so, the misty clouds of greed, anger, and hatred
Continue to extend over the sky of true and real shinjin, or True Reality.

9.
But just as clouds and mists obscure the sunlight,
Brightness, not darkness, prevails under the clouds and mists.
When we are in the grasp of true entrusting—when we realize shinjin— and
    experience the great joy of humbly respecting the Dharma,
We immediately transcend the five evil realms of existence.

10.
All foolish beings, whether good or evil,
Who listen to the Dharma and trust in universal deliverance,
Receive the Buddha's praises as people of great understanding;
Such people are called "pure white lotus flowers."

11.
Nembutsu, emerging from the Innermost Aspiration of Amida Buddha,
Is, for ignorant, arrogant, evil-minded sentient beings,
Extremely difficult to receive joyfully and to hold onto;
Nothing exceeds this most difficult of all difficulties.

12.
The writers of India who wrote treatises explaining the teachings
And wise masters of China and Japan
Revealed the true intent for Śākyamuni Buddha's appearance in the world
And clarified that the Tathāgata's Innermost Aspiration accords with the nature
    of all beings.

13.
In the *Lankāvatāra Sutra*, Śākyamuni Buddha
Predicted to the multitudes that in southern India
A great master called Nāgārjuna would appear in the world
To crush the wrong views of inherent existence and nihilism.

14.
Nāgārjuna expounded the unequaled Mahāyāna teachings
And became a bodhisattva, dwelling in the realm of Peace and Happiness.
He revealed that difficult practices are like walking on the land, thus causing suffering,
But that the easy practice is pleasant, like sailing on water.

15.
When we with total mindfulness ponder Amida's Innermost Aspiration,
We quite naturally and spontaneously enter the stage of being assured of liberation.
Only by constant attention to the recitation of the Tathāgata's Name
Can we express our gratitude for the favor of universal deliverance provided by Great Compassion. [Thus taught Nāgārjuna.]

16.
Bodhisattva Vasubandhu declared in a discourse
That he took refuge in the Tathāgata of Unobstructed Light.
Relying on the sutras, he pointed at True Reality
And clarified the Great Vow by which we leap crosswise beyond birth-and-death.

17.
Amida's directing of virtue in the Original Vow
Revealed the meaning of One Mind in order to emancipate all beings.
When devotees enter the Great Treasure-Ocean of merits,
They are certain to be one with the Great Assembly [of those who have been liberated].

18.
When they reach the Lotus-Storehouse World, or the threshold of liberation,
They will instantly realize *Dharmakāya*, or Thusness.
While cavorting in the forests of blind passions, they will manifest transcendent powers;
Entering samsara, they will assume various forms to guide others [to liberation].
[Thus taught Vasubandhu.]

19.
Venerable Master Donran was revered by the Emperor of Liang,
Who always venerated him as a bodhisattva.
When the *tripitaka* master, Bodhiruci, gave Donran the Pure Land teachings,
Donran burned his Taoist writings and took refuge in the Pure Land doctrine.

20.
In his commentary on the treatise of Bodhisattva Vasubandhu,
He revealed that Amida's Vows are the cause and effect of birth in the Land of Recompense.
Directing of virtue, in its going and returning aspects, originates in Other Power.
True assurance of Buddhahood is attained only through shinjin—or heartfelt entrusting.

21.
When true entrusting is awakened in deluded and defiled foolish beings,
They will instantly realize the non-duality of birth-and-death and nirvāna.
They will most assuredly reach the Land of Immeasurable Light
And will join the process of liberating sentient beings everywhere. [Thus taught Donran.]

22.
Dōshaku emphasized that the Path of Sages is difficult for the attainment of liberation
And declared that the Pure Land Path is the only path to liberation [for foolish beings].
He criticized the numerous self-power practices of good deeds
And encouraged us solely to say the Name containing perfect virtues.

23.
He kindly admonished us to heed the three aspects of entrusting and non-entrusting,
And with great compassion guided all equally, despite the Dharma Age in which they lived.
No matter how many evils we have committed in our lives, if we encounter the Original Vow,
We will reach the Land of Peace and realize the wonderful fruit of enlightenment. [Thus taught Dōshaku.]

24.
Zendō alone in his day clarified the true intent of Śākyamuni Buddha.
Feeling sorrow for those who practice meditative and non-meditative good, as well as those who commit grave offenses,
He revealed that the Light and Name are the cause and condition for birth in the Pure Land.
When true practicers enter the Great Wisdom Ocean of the Original Vow,

25.
They receive the diamond-like mind
And simultaneously experience the immense joy of one thought-moment—
As Vaidehī [in the sutras] acquired great insight—
And instantly realize the eternal bliss of True Reality. [Thus taught Zendō.]

26.
Genshin, having delved deeply into the lifetime teachings of Śākyamuni Buddha,
Chose to follow solely the Pure Land Path and encouraged all to do likewise.
He distinguished between the exclusive practice [of nembutsu] and the shallow path of sundry practices,
Pointing out the differences between various states of attainment, or birth in the fulfilled land or transformed land.

27.
Seekers with the burden of evil karma should simply say the Name,
Realizing that they, too, are embraced by the Light,
And that although their ignorance and blind passions prevent their seeing it,
[The Light of] Great Compassion nonetheless constantly shines on them. [Thus taught Genshin.]

28.
Genkū, the great master [of Pure Land Buddhism], clarified the Buddha's teachings.
Feeling great pity for all foolish beings, both good and evil,
He spread the true teachings and realization to remote areas of Japan
And transmitted the Original Vow to all of us in the defiled world.

29.
Returning to samsara and suffering
Is certainly the result of feelings of doubt.
Our speedy entry into the realm of tranquility and transcendence
Is an inevitable result of the mind of shinjin, or true entrusting. [Thus taught Genkū.]

30.
The great masters who spread the teachings of the Pure Land sutras
Have liberated countless beings in this world of defilement and evil.
All people of the present Age—whether ministers or lay—should with great mindfulness
Place their trust in the teachings of our venerable masters.

[Prose translation by Bob Bolander]

Shōshinge in English Verse (正信偈)
Verses on True Shinjin and Nembutsu

1.
In the Tathāgata of Life Beyond Measure we take refuge and also proclaim
That in the Light Surpassing All Thoughts and Ideas, we joyfully do the same.
Dharmākara while on the bodhisattva path kept strict abidance
And in Lokeśvararāja Buddha he found excellent guidance.

2.
He examined the origins of the Buddhas' pure lands with utmost concentration;
Of everything good and bad in those lands he made full observation.
The Original Vows of great deliverance became articulated,
And his unsurpassed and highest Aspiration emanated.

3.
After timeless and deep concentration, he was undeterred
From making the Vow that everywhere his many names be heard:
Light Beyond All Measure, Light Unbounded and Unconfined,
Light Unhindered, Light Unequaled, Light of all Brilliances Combined,

4.
Light That Is Pure, Light That Is Joyful, Light of Wisdom Flowing,
Light Unceasing, Light Beyond All Words, Beyond All Knowing,
And Light Surpassing the Sun and Moon. These Lights shine everywhere—
On all the worlds and likewise on all sentient beings wheresoe'er.

5.
Our truly settled state is the Vow of Amida Buddha's Name;
Through the mind of true and sincere entrusting to Buddhahood we aim.
The highest bodhisattva stage—our enlightened situation—
Without a doubt fulfills the Vow of our ultimate liberation.

6.
Śākyamuni Buddha did on this very Earth appear
To make Amida's Innermost Aspiration utterly clear.
We multitudes of beings who reside in times of great defilements
Should trust in the truth of the Buddha's words and thus avoid beguilements.

7.
One thought-moment of joy emerges from our deep contemplation,
And without the severing of our blind passions we gain liberation.
Foolish and wise offenders of the Dharma, who by the grasp of the Vow are graced,
Resemble the rivers that on entering the ocean transform into one salty taste.

8.
The light of all-embracing Compassion shines on us always—it's true—
Protecting us all as though the darkness of ignorance has already been broken through;
Even so, extending over the sky of true shinjin are cautions that we must heed:
The vast, misty clouds of anger and hatred and selfish desire and greed.

9.
But just as the darkness of clouds and mists obscures the light of the sun,
Below the clouds we can still see the light, for the brightness cannot be undone.
When in the grasp of joyful entrusting our humble reverence is deep,
Over the five evil realms of existence we crosswise and instantly leap.

10.
All foolish beings who are living on earth and whether they're evil or good
And trust in the great universal deliverance—striving for sure Buddhahood—
As excellent people of vast understanding by the Buddha are acclaimed;
Such people, in fact, *puṇḍarīkas*—or white lotus flowers—are named.

11.
Nembutsu rightly embodies the Buddha Amida's Original Vow,
And for evil-minded, ignorant, and arrogant beings it certainly still proves now
Very hard to receive with deep trusting joy and difficult also to hold;
Of all of life's challenges, this one must be the most difficult one, we are told.

12.
The writers of India wrote texts on the teachings, explaining each word one by one,
As well as the masters of the Middle Kingdom and the Land of the Rising Sun.
The true intent for the appearance of Śākyamuni, the Sage, they made plain;
They also revealed that to people of all Ages the Vows of Amida pertain.

13.
Long ago on Mount Lanka, Śākyamuni the Tathāgata foretold—the scriptures do
    say—
To multitudes of followers listening intently that far off in the future one day
A great noble master, Nāgārjuna by name, would surely in this world appear,
To make all the views on both being and non-being strikingly, perfectly clear.

14.
The marvelous Mahāyāna teachings Nāgārjuna clearly expounded,
And eventually he attained the stage of Peace and Bliss unbounded.
He said that difficult practice was like our walking on land, which can be
Very hard; while easy practice was likened to sailing on a smooth, gentle sea.

15.
When we grasp with total mindfulness Amida's Innermost Aspiration,
We enter the definitely settled stage without any hesitation.
By keeping our focus on the Tathāgata's Name with a sincere and trusting
    attitude,
We express to the Great Compassionate Vow our deep and heartfelt gratitude.

16.
In treatises did the great Bodhisattva Vasubandhu write
That he himself took refuge in the Buddha of Unimpeded Light;
Relying on the *Larger Sutra*, he declared that crosswise we
Transcend samsara by the Great Vow to realize True Reality.

17.
The power of the Vow and Amida's transference of merits form the core
Of the manifestation of the One Mind to guide all beings to the other shore.
When entering the Great Treasure-Ocean of merits all seekers for certain are
    bound
For the Pure Land Path, where those of the Great Assembly are to be found.

18.
On reaching the Lotus-Storehouse World, or the threshold of true liberation,
They instantly realize *Dharmakāya*, or total emancipation.
Beset with blind passions, they will manifest transcendent potentiality
And in various forms return to lead others to ultimate reality.

19.
Donran was greatly revered by Emperor Liang of the Chinese nation,
And he as a bodhisattva received the emperor's veneration.
When from Bodhiruci to Donran the Pure Land teachings came,
Embracing the Doctrine, he completely destroyed his Taoist works with a flame.

20.
Donran, in his comments on Vasubandhu, said that it made perfect sense
That the Vows are the cause and effect of our birth in the Land of Recompense.
The directing of virtue—its going and returning—is Other Power's endurance:
Through shinjin—or heartfelt entrusting—comes the stage of Right Assurance.

21.
That true entrusting is awakened in foolish beings is Amida's *dāna*,
For we instantly realize that birth-and-death is identical to nirvāna;
On reaching the Land of Immeasurable Light we most assuredly share
In the process of liberating all sentient beings in all places—everywhere.

22.
Dōshaku said that by the Path of the Sages enlightenment is hard to attain;
The Pure Land Path is the only path to enter liberation's domain.
He criticized harshly the self-power practice of trying to do the good deed
And urged us to focus on Amida's Name, which is true virtue's wonderful seed.

23.
Three aspects of faith—of both pure and impure—he kindly explicated;
He has guided all seekers—Dharma Age notwithstanding—with Compassion unabated.
On encountering the Innermost Aspiration, though our misconduct has found no surcease,
We will realize true liberation when we reach the Land of Peace.

24.
Zendō alone wanted to clarify the Buddha's true intent,
And pitying self-power practicers and beings whose lives in evil are spent,
He taught that the Light and the Name are the cause and condition for their Pure Land birth.
He said when they enter the Great Wisdom Ocean of the Original Vow's real worth

25.
And at the same time experience the joy of one thought-moment, they will find
That they, too, have received the indestructible Diamond Mind;
To them the bliss of True Reality instantly will unfold—
As threefold insight came to Vaidehi in the stories and sutras of old.

26.
Genshin deeply delved into the Buddha's teachings from the distant past,
And solely of the Path of the Pure Land he became an enthusiast.
Setting apart true practice from acts that sundry practices demand,
He showed the difference between our birth in the Transformed versus Recompensed Land.

27.
By saying the Name with a trusting heart, the seekers will know that despite
Their heavy karmic burdens, they are embraced by Amida's Light.
Though they are unaware because of blind passions and burdensome karma,
On them Great Compassion continues to shine—the Light of Buddha Dharma.

28.
Master Genkū studied Buddhist teachings as thoroughly as he could.
He felt great pity for all foolish beings—for the evil and also the good.
To distant regions of Japan the Pure Land teachings he unfurled
And transmitted Amida's Original Vow to all in the defiled world.

29.
Continuing the cycle of birth-and-death, or samsara, comes about
Certainly as a result of the ties that bind us to feelings of doubt.
But entering the realm of uncreated tranquility or quiet transcendence,
Results from the mind of true entrusting and the grasping of interdependence.

30.
The masters who spread the Pure Land teachings throughout the world all sought
To liberate countless beings, who in the world of defilement were caught.
With mindfulness should all, both ministers and lay, who live in the present Age,
Place complete trust in the exquisite teachings of each respectable Sage.

[Verse translation by Bob Bolander]

Singing

Amida's Gift

(*Amida's Paradise*)

Rev. Bob Oshita and
Tacoma Buddhist Temple Gatha Committee

Arr. by C. Iwanaga

Singing

Amida's Guiding Light

Tacoma Buddhist Temple Gatha Committee Donna Sasaki

Singing

jes - tic moun - tain chains, hop - ing some - day to
til the light comes shin - ing through. Then we see the
ter - nal grat - i - tude, we find a life of

know Nir - va - na's peace - ful plains.
answer and come to know what's true.
faith in full - ness and qui - e - tude.

Sung after verse 3

Na - mo A - mi - da Bu - tsu.

Amida's Shrine
(At Our Altar)

Mieko Takamiya
Revised by OCBC

Osamu Shimizu

Moderato

1. Each morn-ing I a-wake to see, A— mi-da's face so good and kind. I think he says good morn-ing child. He's glad to start the day with me.
2. Each night be-fore I go to bed, I— sit be-fore A-mi-da's shrine with pret-ty flow-ers, can-dle light, and in-cense curl-ing round my head.
3. I bow my head, I clasp my hands, and— thank Bud-dha with all my might for teach-ings that will bring Truth's light to peo-ple all a-cross this land.

Asa no Uta

(*Morning Song*)

Daigu Sugisaki
Trans. by Hawaii Committee and OCBC

Yasuo Suehiro

Awaken in Amida's Light

Wendie Yumori

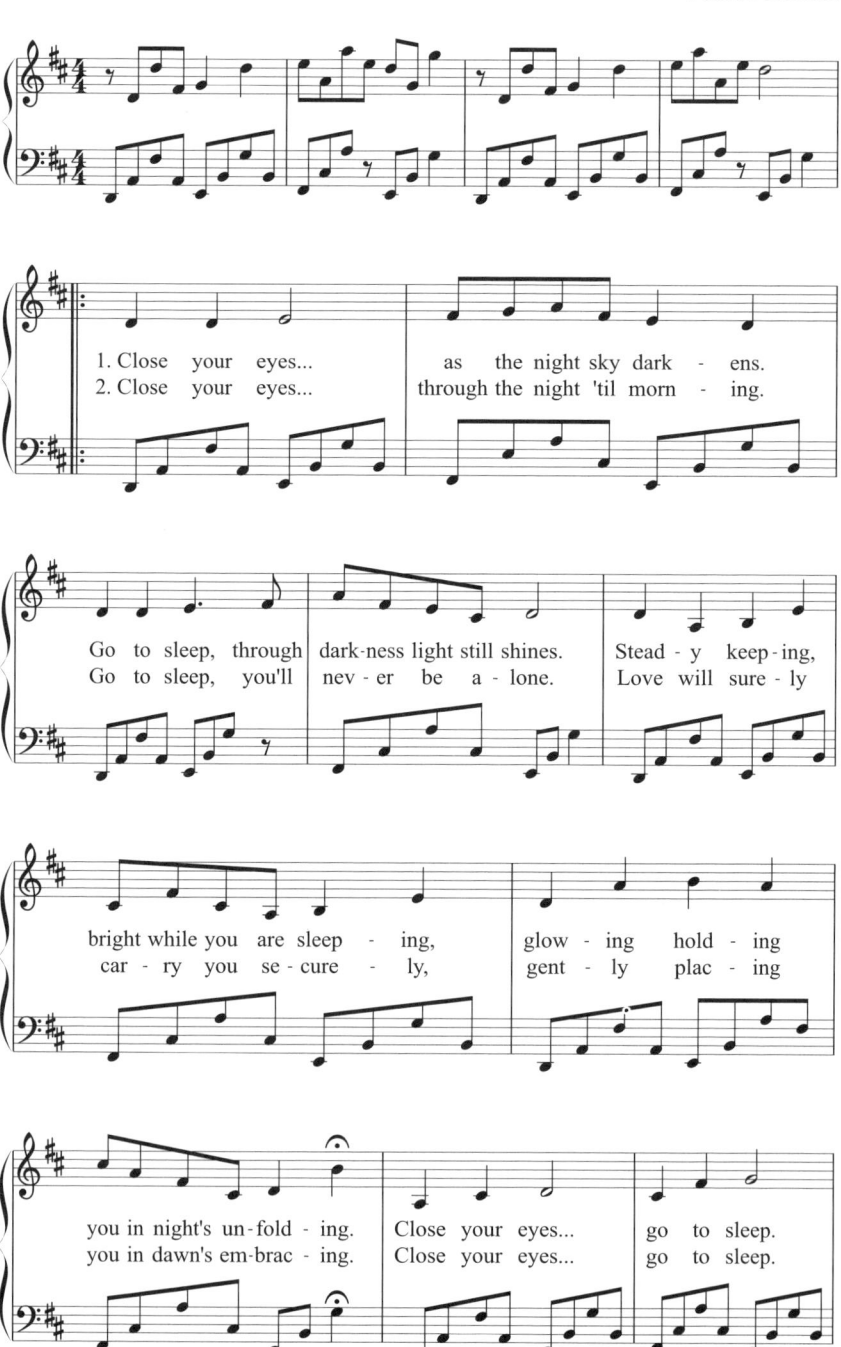

1. Close your eyes... as the night sky darkens. Go to sleep, through darkness light still shines. Steady keeping, bright while you are sleeping, you in night's unfolding. Close your eyes... go to sleep.
2. Close your eyes... through the night 'til morning. Go to sleep, you'll never be alone. Love will surely carry you securely, gently placing you in dawn's embracing. Close your eyes... go to sleep.

Evening Gatha

D. Hunt
Revised by OCBC

H. M. Uyeda

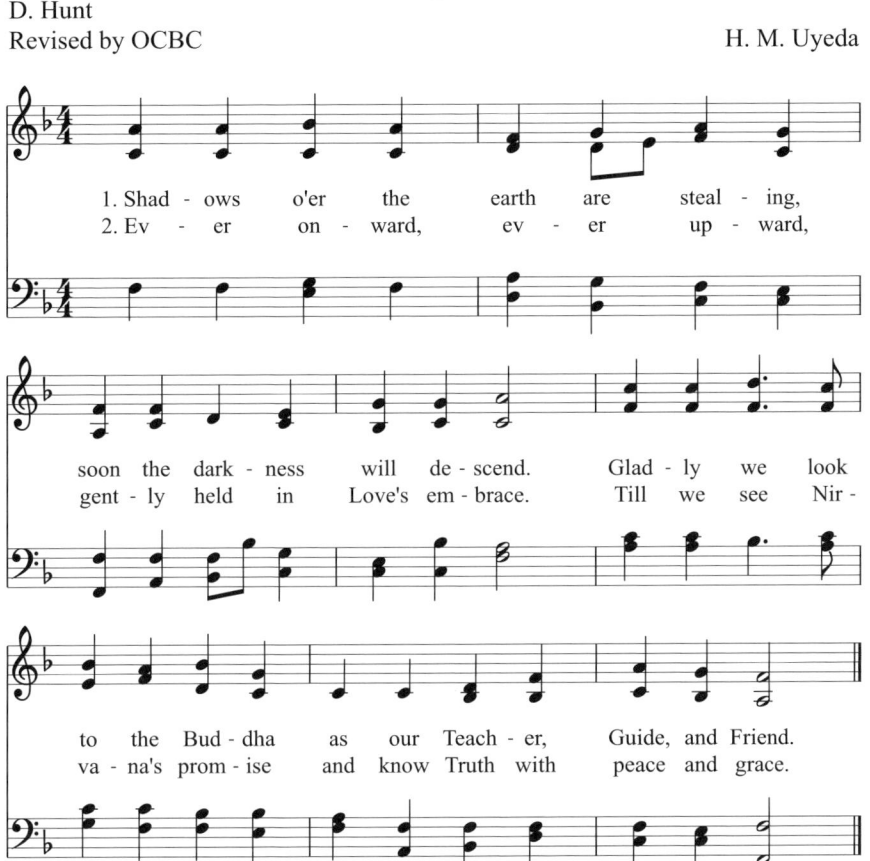

1. Shad - ows o'er the earth are steal - ing, soon the dark - ness will de - scend. Glad - ly we look to the Bud - dha as our Teach - er, Guide, and Friend.
2. Ev - er on - ward, ev - er up - ward, gent - ly held in Love's em - brace. Till we see Nir - vana's prom - ise and know Truth with peace and grace.

Falling Leaves

From Ryōkan's haiku on...

With gassho to Rev. A. Miyaji

R. Maruyama

The Zen monk Ryōkan lived a very simple life, and stories about his kindness and generosity abound. This song is based on a poem that he composed on his deathbed:

うらを見せ　おもてを見せて　散るもみじ
ura o mise / omote o misete / chiru momiji

Farewell

Kimi Hisatsune
Revised by OCBC

Jane Imamura

1. Now we've heard the Dhar - ma for an - oth - er day. Let us gath - er 'round the shrine, bow our heads and say: thank you, sen - sei, for your help, thank you ev - ery - one. Bud - dha's love will keep us safe till our work is done.

2. So we'll meet a - gain next week, won't you take good care? Let us try to do what's right, al - ways kind and fair. We shall spread the hap - pi - ness faith in Bud - dha brings. Now it's time to say good-bye till we meet a - gain.

3. Na - mo A - mi - da Bu - tsu, sing this fine re - frain. Na - mo A - mi - da Bu - tsu, sun - ny day or rain. Na - mo A - mi - da Bu - tsu, strong in faith re - main. Na - mo A - mi - da Bu - tsu, till we meet a - gain.

Fundarike
(Lotus Flowers)

Seikichi Kawakami Kosaku Yamada

Gassho, 'Round the World

Michiko Yukawa
Donna Sasaki

Hanamatsuri

(Flower Festival)

Hongwanji Shakaibu Senka

S. Fujii
Arr. by C. Iwanaga

1. Wa ta shi no su - ki na zo - no i ru, i - n do no ku - ni no ha na zo no de. O u ma re na sa re ta o sha ka sa ma, kyo - o wa to o to i ha na ma tsu ri.

2. Ki re i na ha - na o tsu mi ma sho o, o ka za ri shi ma sho o ha na mi do o. Mi ho to ke sa - ma ni te o a wa su, kyo - o wa u re shi i ha na ma tsu ri.

Hanamatsuri Kodomo no Uta
(Children's Song for Hanamatsuri)

Minoru Kainuma
Trans. by Hawaii Music Committee and OCBC

Isamu Tateno

Singing

Happy Little Children

Revised F. Blanning-Pooley

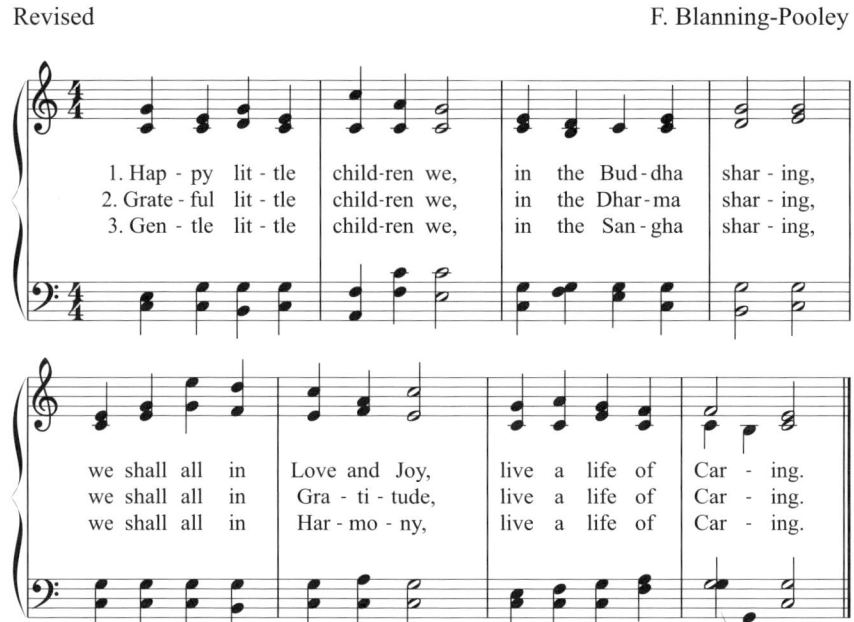

1. Hap-py lit-tle child-ren we, in the Bud-dha shar-ing,
2. Grate-ful lit-tle child-ren we, in the Dhar-ma shar-ing,
3. Gen-tle lit-tle child-ren we, in the San-gha shar-ing,

we shall all in Love and Joy, live a life of Car-ing.
we shall all in Gra-ti-tude, live a life of Car-ing.
we shall all in Har-mo-ny, live a life of Car-ing.

Hotoke no Kodomo
(Children of Amida)

Guhan Akita
Trans. by OCBC

Yasuo Sawa

1. Wa - re-ra wa ho - to-ke no ko - do-mo na ri.
2. Wa - re-ra wa ho - to-ke no ko - do-mo na ri.
3. Each of us is like a child of Ho - to-ke sa - ma.

U - re-shi to - ki mo, ka - na-shi to ki mo,
O - sa-na ki to - ki mo, o - i ta ru to - ki mo,
When our hearts are full of cheer, when we are in deep de-spair,

mi o-ya no so - de ni su - ga-ri nan.
mi o-ya ni ka wa - ra zu tsu ka - e nan.
trust-ing-ly we look to A-mi da. He is al-ways there.

Singing 117

In Lumbini's Garden

Paul Carus
Revised by OCBC

R.R. Bode

1. Soft-ly blew the breez-es, on that glo-ri-ous morn, in Lum-bi-ni's gar-den where Sid-dhar-tha was born.
2. From the earth sprang flow-ers, birds in war-bles sang, through the earth and the heav-ens strains of mu-sic rang.
3. Gods and men and an-gels, all for wor-ship came, glo-ry to Sid-dhar-tha, glo-ry to his Name.

I'm a Link in the Golden Chain

Gordon Ah Tye
Co-arranger Janet Tamura

Copyright 2004 by Gordon Ah Tye

Infinite Love and Wisdom

(*To accompany the Golden Chain*)

Ancient Chant R.R. Bode

It's Raining

Kimi Hisatsune

Jane Imamura

Singing

Joyful in Amida's Light

Donna Sasaki

Kiyokeki Hikari

(清光, *Pure Light*)

Shinran Shonin
Osamu Hidaka

1. Mi - da - jo-u bu-tsu no ko no ka ta wa, i ma ni jik - ko-u o he ta ma e ri. Ho - o shi-n no ko-u ri-n ki wa mo na - ku,
2. Chi e no ko-u — myo-u ha ka ri na shi, u ryo no sho so-u ko to — go to ku. Ko - u ke u ka mu ra nu mo no wa na - shi,
3. Sho-u — jo-u ko-u — myo-u na ra bi na shi, gu shi ko-u no yu e na re ba. Is - sa - i no gok — ke mo no zo ko ri — nu,

Singing

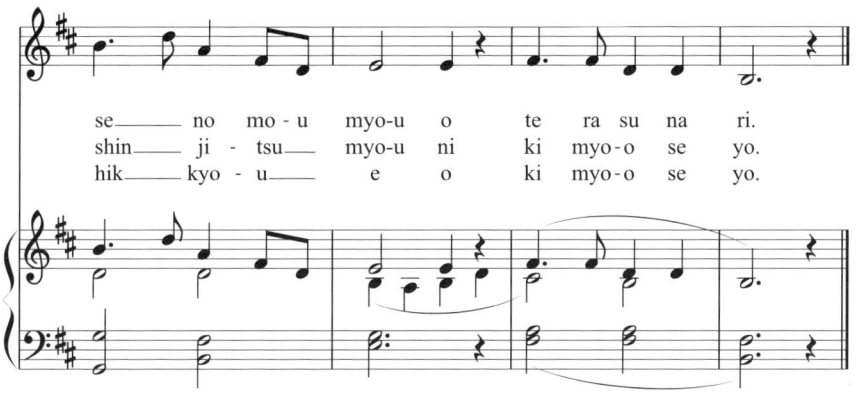

1.
Amida has passed through ten kalpas now
Since realizing Buddhahood;
Dharma-body's wheel of light is without bound,
Shining on the blind and ignorant of the world.

2.
The light of wisdom exceeds all measure,
And every finite living being
Receives this illumination that is like the dawn,
So take refuge in Amida, the true and real light.

3.
The light of purity is without compare.
When a person encounters this light,
All bonds of karma fall away;
So take refuge in Amida, the ultimate shelter.

From The Collected Works of Shinran, Vol. 1,
© 1997 Jōdo Shinshū Hongwanji-ha, pp. 325-326.

In the course of his life, Shinran went by at least six different names. Born into the Hino family in 1173, his given name was Matsuwakamaru. He received the name Hannen upon becoming a Tendai monk in 1181. During the years of study with Hōnen, he adopted the names Shakkū, Zenshin, and finally Shinran to reflect his deepening understanding of the Pure Land teachings. While in exile, and for the rest of his life, he added the name Gutoku (foolish, stubble-haired one) to signify his break with institutional Buddhism.

Maru Sankaku Shikaku
(Circle, Triangle, Rectangle)

Hiroshi Sashikata
Trans. by Rev. Noriaki Ito

Hiroki & Tomoko Wada
Arr. by OCBC

1. Ma - ru san-ka-ku shi - ka - ku, ma - ru san-ka-ku shi - ka - ku.
2. Cir - cle tri-an-gle rec - tan-gle, cir - cle tri-an-gle rec - tan-gle.
3. Cir - cle tri-an-gle rec - tan-gle, cir - cle tri-an-gle rec - tan-gle.

Ka - o mo ka - ta - chi mo chi - ga - u ke - do,
Fac - es and bod - ies come in diff'-rent shapes and shades,
Dreams and hopes may all be ve - ry dif - fer - ent,

da - ka - ra to - te - mo o - mo-shi-ro - i. Do - ki na
but that's what makes life so in - ter-est - ing. All em-braced in
but that's what makes life so won - der-ful. With the gift of

Reprinted by permission of Los Angeles Higashi Honganji Betsuin.

Mihotoke ni Idakarete
(Embraced by Amida)

Nichiyo School Assn.
Trans. by OCBC

Seijin Nomura
Arr. by Kiyomi Fujii

Mihotoke wa
(*Amida Buddha*)

Ryoichi Nakano
Kiyoshi Nobutoki

1. The worldly ties have ended.
But our departed friend in Dharma
Finds happiness in Amida's presence.
In our sadness, there is consolation.

2. Parting from this sad, grieving world,
Our friend is born into a happier world
To become a wondrous Buddha.
In our grief, there is consolation.

Namo Amida Butsu

Shinkaku
R. R. Bode

Andante

1. When life is fair and sun-light gilds the day, when for-tune smiles and flow'rs a-dorn our way, oft let us pause with grate-ful hearts to say,
2. E'en though our way leads 'neath a dark-en'd sky, and to our loved ones pain and death draw nigh, our tears may flow, yet trust-ing-ly we cry,

Na - mo A - mi - da Bu - tsu.

Nembutsu I

Chizu Iwanaga

Nembutsu II

Osamu Shimizu

Nichiyobi
(Joyful Sunday)

Seiya Kai
Trans. by OCBC

Yasuo Sawa

Now We See

R. Maruyama

1. So many roses in other gardens,
So much good fortune in other lives.
Ah, did you see the love that surrounds you?
See how we bask in a simple good life.
Now we see through Buddha's great

2. Look at his mansion, his fame and his fortune,
Why is he so lucky in love and in life?
Ah, did you see the things he's forsaken?
Choices were made for this path long ago.
Now we see through Buddha's great

3. So many years of study and learning,
See how the words and quotations do flow.
But, are the lessons just black print on paper?
Let's bow our heads in earnest gassho.
Now we see through Buddha's great

Ondokusan (恩徳讃)

(In Praise of Benevolence)

如来大悲の恩徳は
(にょらいだいひのおんどくは)

身を粉にしても報ずべし
(みをこにしてもほうずべし)

師主知識の恩徳も
(ししゅちしきのおんどくも)

ほねをくだきても謝すべし
(ほねをくだきてもしゃすべし)

Such is the benevolence of the Tathāgata's great compassion,
That I must strive to repay it even if my body turns to dust;
Such is the benevolence of the masters and true teachers,
That I will thank them until my bones have crumbled.

Ondokusan is one of Shinran's Japanese-language poems about the Last Dharma Age (*mappō*). The subject of these poems is our inability to attain enlightenment through the mind of self-power. Shinran praises the benevolence of Śākyamuni Buddha and the seven Pure Land masters who guide us to awaken through the power-beyond-the-self. Nothing I might do, "even if my body turns to dust," is sufficient to repay my debt to them.

Ondokusan I
(*In Praise of Benevolence*)

Shinran Shonin — Yasuo Sawa

Ondokusan II

Shinran Shonin
Osamu Shimizu

Path of Nembutsu

Tacoma Buddhist Temple Gatha Committee

Donna Sasaki

1. Walk a-long the Path of Nem-bu-tsu, fol-low-ing in Shin-ran's foot-steps true, lis-ten to the call of A-mi-da, Na-mo A-mi-da Bu-tsu. Na-mo A-mi-da Bu, Na-mo A-mi-da Bu-tsu.

2. Though we some-times strug-gle day to day, feel-ing loss or things don't go our way, lis-ten to the call of A-mi-da, Na-mo A-mi-da Bu-tsu.

Raisan-ka

(Reverence and Praise)

Trans. by Senshin Buddhist Temple

Seishin Fujii

Singing

1. Just as there is no corner where the light does not shine, so too is the broad and all-embracing nature of the Dharma Vow. —Myonyo Shonin

2. The effect of the Vow is great, there is no corner of the world where it does not reach. —Ohtani Kazuko

3. How tranquil! The enjoyment of this single day, in the presence of the Buddha, of a certainty, not excluded. —Ohtani Kinuko

4. Like the Great Phoenix who parts the clouds in flight, I am priviledged to be enabled to spread the Buddha's teachings. —Ohtani Yoshiko

5. Ah, we, without knowing our own evils from birth to birth, world to world; before the eyes of Compassion, how can we be so self-indulgent? —Kujo Takeko

Sayonara

Teiin Hatano
Trans. by OCBC

Takushin Kushi

1. Ta no shi ku kyo mo su mi ma shi ta.
2. Sa-yo-na-ra mi na sa - n go ki ge - n yo.
3. Sa-yo-na-ra to our friends, please stay safe and well.

Ya sa shi mi o ya ni ma mo ra re te.
Sa - yo-na - ra se - n se - i o da - i ji ni.
Sa - yo-na - ra se - n se - i, you must take good care.

U re shi o u chi e ka e ri ma sho.
Ta no shi ko - n do no tsu do i ma de.
You are all in my thoughts un - til we meet a - gain.

Seiya
(Sacred Night)

Takeko Kujo
Trans. by Hawaii Committee

Shimpei Nakayama

Andante

1. Ho - shi no yo zo - ra no u - tsu ku - shi sa, ta re ka - wa shi ru ya a - me no na zo.
2. Splen - dor of an eve - ning sky filled with count - less stars, who can ev - er fath - om its time - less mys - te - ry?
3. More than all the count - less sands Gan - ges Ri - ver holds, are the in - fi - nite Bud - dhas who fill this u - ni - verse,

Mu su - no hi - to mi
Millions of lights, when spark - ling bright,
ev - er watch - ful o - ver us,

Singing

Shinransama

Tsuneharu Takita
Trans. by OCBC

Yuji Koseki

1. So yo ka ze wa ta ru a sa no ma do, ha ta ra ku te no hi ra a wa se tsu tsu. Na-mo A-mi-
2. Win-dow o-pen to the dawn, gen-tle bree-zes blow. Hands to-geth-er mind-ful-ly, then to my work I go. Na-mo A-mi-
3. Glit-ter-ing, the light of stars in the eve-ning sky, Fades a-way from my sight when clouds and mist roll by. Na-mo A-mi-

Singing

The Chanting of the Sutras

Sus Iwamasa
R. Maruyama

Singing

chant-ing of the Su-tras will help me see. The Nem-bu-tsu will set me
chant-ing of the Su-tras will help us see. The Nem-bu-tsu will set us

Na - mo A - mi - da Bu-

Na - mo A - mi - da

1. free.
2. free. Gan ni shi ku do-ku, Byo-do sei is-sai, Do ho-

tsu   tsu

tsu bo-dai shin, O-jo___ a___ n rak-ko-ku. *8va*

Tsuki ga Deta
(The Moon Has Risen)

Nichiyo School Association
Trans. by OCBC

Seijin Nomura

1. Tsu - ki ga de - ta, tsu - ki ga de - ta. Te ma ri no yo - o ni ma - n ma ru ku. Mi - ho - to - ke sa - ma no o ko - ko - ro wa, tsu - ki no yo - o ni ma - n ma - ru i.
2. Tsu - ki ga de - ta, tsu - ki ga de - ta. Ka ga mi no yo - o ni ku mo ra zu ni. Mi - ho - to - ke sa - ma no o ko - ko - ro wa, tsu - ki no yo - o ni ku - mo ra na i.
3. The moon has ris - en, ris - en in the sky. Light of great com - pas - sion guides me on my way. The heart of A - mi — da, shin - ing like the moon, is full of beau - ty and se - ren - i - ty.

Vandana Ti-Sarana

(Homage and Three Refuges) Ancient Chant

With Grateful Hearts
(I Love the Story)

Rev. Bob Oshita
Yumi Hojo
Arr. by OCBC

1. Each week we come to Dharma School, we Gassho and say Nembutsu. With grateful hearts and minds we say Namo Amida Butsu.
2. Each day we wake in gratitude, that is a life of Nembutsu. With grateful hearts and minds we say Namo Amida Butsu.
3. Each night we sleep in harmony, for all the world is one with me. With grateful hearts and minds we say Namo Amida Butsu.

With These Hands

Mieko Takamiya
Toshiro Mayuzumi

Notes

Shinran's Path

Shinran expressed his two-part life story this way: "Reflecting within myself, I see that in the various teachings of the Path of Sages, practice and enlightenment died out long ago, and that Jōdo Shinshū is the path to realization that is now vital and flourishing."

"Reflecting within myself" emphasizes that Shinran's path was one of self-examination, and that the statements to follow are autobiographical. They express what was dead and what was flourishing in him.

"I see that in the various teachings of the Path of Sages, practice and enlightenment died out long ago." Shinran's early life as a monk was devoted to the Path of Sages. It included extreme physical and mental practices similar to those followed by Siddhārtha prior to his awakening. This phase of Shinran's life came to an end when he, like Siddhārtha, reached an impasse and discarded the approach he had relied on.

"I see that Jōdo Shinshū is the path to realization that is now vital and flourishing." The words Jōdo (pure land) and Shinshū (true essence) mean that, for Shinran, the Pure Land Path is the true essence of Buddhism. He entered this path by listening to his teacher Hōnen, who embodied the timeless truth of the Dharma. Upon receiving the Dharma from Hōnen, Shinran stopped relying on his religious ego, and instead became a truth seeker like Dharmākara, the hero of the story told in the *Larger Sutra*. Although he continued to revere Hōnen as his great teacher, Shinran went beyond Hōnen's teachings as he deepened his understanding of the Dharma. And so, Shinran's path to realization remained vital and flourishing.

To learn more about the key events on Shinran's path, see *The Collected Works of Shinran*, Vol. 1, © 1997 Jōdo Shinshū Hongwanji-ha, pp. 289-291.

Shinran's Teaching

Prior to Shinran it was understood that we must perform good practices and, with a sincere mind, direct our virtues toward birth in the Pure Land. Shinran saw himself as incapable of any such virtuous actions. Instead, the directing of virtue (*ekō*) was solely from the mind of Amida to him. Shinran taught that the fulfillment of Vow 18 in the *Larger Sutra* enables foolish beings to realize a life of awakening or shinjin. His re-interpretation of the Vow's fulfillment is paraphrased as follows:

Sho u shu jō	All living beings
Mon go myō gō	hear the meaning of Namo Amida Butsu
Shin jin kan gi	and realize shinjin and joy
Nai shi ichi nen	in one timeless moment
Shi shin e kō	when the sincere mind of Amida awakens
Gan shō hi koku	their aspiration for birth in that land.
Soku toku ō jō	Immediately, they attain birth
Jū fu tai ten	and dwell in the stage of non-retrogression.
Yui jo go gyaku	Only those committing the five grave offenses
Hi hō shō bō	and slandering the true Dharma are excluded.

Shinran taught that "birth" and "the stage of non-retrogression" occur immediately when shinjin is realized, which means that the eventual attainment of Buddhahood is assured. Remarkably, he emphasized the exclusion statement of Vow 18 and saw himself as committing grave offenses and slandering the Dharma. Thus, the exclusion statement is an activity of Amida's sincere mind revealing what I truly am – a foolish being lacking any capacity for good, who is therefore the Vow's true object of liberation.

For a glossary of Shin Buddhist terms, please see *The Three Pure Land Sutras* (2009) Vol. II, pp. 105-116. For Shinran's interpretation of the *Larger Sutra*, see *The Collected Works of Shinran*, Vol. 2, pp. 145-148.

Types of Services and Observances

Meditation
Meditation is being incorporated in Shin Buddhist temples in a variety of ways, as a preparation for listening to the Buddha-Dharma. Some temples hold meditation services in addition to family service. Other temples use meditation as a quiet moment of reflection within their family service. For still others, meditation is not a part of the temple routine.

Family or Regular Service
The family or regular service is conventionally held on Sunday, although Sunday holds no special significance in Buddhism. The service is conducted primarily in English, although certain readings, songs, and Dharma talks are sometimes in Japanese. The service includes group readings, sutra chanting, Dharma talks, and the singing of *gathas* (Buddhist songs). Many temples also provide Dharma School for children and study classes for adults.

Special Services

The format of special services is similar to the format of regular service, with the addition of a pronouncement (*hyōbyakumon*) declaring the purpose of the gathering, special attire for the ministers, and added adornments to the onaijin. Some observances are marked by a ritual that is specific to the day. The Dharma talk may be given by a guest speaker. Otoki, a shared meal, follows most special services. Some of these special days, such as the birth of Śākyamuni, are common to all Buddhist traditions, while others are specific to Shin Buddhism. Services are held on a Sunday close to the historical date, with the exception of New Year's Day and New Year's Eve services, which are held on the actual date.

Jan 1	New Year's Day	*Shūshō-e*
Jan 16	Shinran Shōnin's Memorial	*Hō-onkō*
Feb 15	Nirvāna Day – Buddha's *Parinirvāna*	*Nehan-e*
Mar 21	Ohigan – Spring Equinox	*Shunki higan-e*
Apr 8	Hanamatsuri – Buddha's Birth	*Kanbutsu-e*
May 21	Shinran Shōnin's Birth	*Gōtan-e*
July	First Obon service after loved one passes	*Hatsubon*
July 15	Obon – Gathering of Joy	*Kangi-e*
Sept 23	Ohigan – Autumn Equinox	*Shūki higan-e*
Nov	Perpetual Sutras Memorial	*Eitaikyō*
Nov	All Life-Forms Service	
Dec	Eshinni's and Kakushinni's Memorial	
Dec 8	Bodhi Day – Buddha's Awakening	*Jōdō-e*
Dec 31	New Year's Eve	*Joya-e*

Other Special Services:
       Infant Presentation   *Hatsumairi / Shosanshiki*
       Affirmation Rites   *Ti-sarana / Kieshiki*

Descriptions of Special Services

January 1: New Year's Day – *Shūshō-e*
Shin Buddhism views New Year's Day as a time to reflect and, with renewed dedication, to endeavor to live a life of gratitude and joy. New Year's Day service originated in Japan during the Nara period (710-794 CE). This service is held during the morning on January 1.

January 16: Shinran Shōnin's Memorial Day – *Hō-onkō*
This observance marks the death of Shinran, the founder of Shin Buddhism. Hō-onkō literally means "Dharma gathering for acknowledging indebtedness" and is observed by many Buddhist traditions to honor their founding masters. Our service includes the chanting of Shōshinge, verses written by Shinran that summarize his teachings.

Rennyo Shōnin urged us to reflect deeply on Shinran's teachings at this time. Rennyo explained that the significance of Hō-onkō is to resolve the problem of shinjin – the entrusting heart – and to become keenly aware of the dilemma of our "birth and death." Realizing shinjin is of paramount importance and is the essence of acknowledging our indebtedness to Shinran.

February 15: Nirvāna Day – Buddha's *Parinirvāna* – *Nehan-e*
Śākyamuni awakened to Truth and became a Buddha at the age of 35. After sharing the Dharma for the next 45 years, he attained perfect enlightenment or *parinirvāna* with his death at age eighty. Nirvāna Day is one of three observances commemorating Śākyamuni, the other two being his birthday on April 8 and his awakening on December 8.

The death of Śākyamuni underscores the teaching of impermanence – the idea that we, and all other beings and things in this world, are subject to constant change. It was the Buddha's intent that through his teachings we would understand the transitory nature of our existence, and ultimately experience Truth.

March 21: Ohigan – Spring Equinox – *Shunki higan-e*

Ohigan services occur twice a year around the spring and fall equinox when the daylight and nighttime are equal. In many ancient cultures, it was a time of celebration to remind us of our deep connection to the rhythms and cycles of the earth and, by extension, to the whole universe.

Ohigan translates as "the other shore" and is a metaphor for crossing from this shore of ignorance, anger, and greed to the other shore of nirvāna and peace. It is a time to reflect on the nature of our true self, which is hidden deeply beneath our ego self. As Shin Buddhists we are part of the larger Mahāyāna tradition that teaches the path of the bodhisattva – a path followed by a person who has the aspiration to become a Buddha. The path includes six activities called *pāramitās*, a Sanskrit word that means "arriving at the other shore." The activities of generosity, discipline, patience, energy, meditation, and insight are said to be transformative because they allow us to transcend the narrow perspective of the ego self.

Arriving at the other shore of nirvāna is a teaching that contains a paradox. A bodhisattva perceives reality-as-it-is by not attaching to divisions between self and other, good and evil, samsara and nirvāna, or the world of duality. Although the Buddhist scriptures speak of crossing from samsara to the other shore, one's arrival consists of realizing that there is no other shore at some distance from samsara. We make a journey to the "pure land" and arrive when we understand that we were there all along.

April 8: Hanamatsuri – Buddha's Birth – *Kanbutsu-e*
This service celebrates the birth of Siddhārtha Gautama, who became Śākyamuni, the historical Buddha. Although this service is popularly called Hanamatsuri (flower festival) in Japanese, the more proper name is *Kanbutsu-e* (bathe-Buddha-gathering), in reference to the ritual of pouring sweet tea over a statue of the baby Buddha. The pouring of tea represents the gentle rain, perfumed by flower petals, that was said to have fallen in Lumbini Garden when Siddhārtha was born. Hanamatsuri is a visually memorable occasion because of the beautifully decorated flower-pavilion (*hanamido*) used to shelter the baby Buddha statue.

The appearance of a Buddha in the world is an extremely rare event, and therefore the era in which we live is auspicious for receiving the Dharma. We have been given a remarkable opportunity to have received life in human form and to listen to the teachings of Śākyamuni, 2500 years after his birth.

May 21: Shinran Shōnin's Birth – *Gōtan-e*
This service celebrates the birth of Shin Buddhism's founder. *Gōtan-e* means "coming-down-birthday-gathering." Another name for this occasion is Fujimatsuri (wisteria festival). The double-wisteria crest is the emblem of Nishi Hongwanji, our mother temple in Kyoto, Japan. The pendant wisteria is a vine that needs the support of a structure in order to bloom, symbolically representing humans who need the support of others. The downward-hanging wisteria flower suggests humility and sincere reverence to Amida.

Shinran's life and teachings represent one of the most significant developments in the history of Buddhism. Before then only the privileged and priests received spiritual instruction. Shinran Shōnin taught that even the poor rice farmer is embraced by the Buddha's infinite light and compassion, and the truth of the Dharma and shinjin awakening are accessible to everyone without discrimination.

Shinran was born in 1173 CE and lived a life of profound spiritual depth. Although we give him the name Shōnin (great teacher), he called himself Gutoku, meaning "unshaven ignorant one," and he looked deeply into his own heart and mind in his search for truth.

He said, "I know truly how grievous it is that I, Gutoku Shinran, am sinking in an immense ocean of desires and attachments and am lost in vast mountains of fame and advantage."

Through his revolutionary understanding of the Dharma, Shinran awakened to a deep appreciation of life's wisdom and compassion that embrace each of us here and now, just as we are. In that realization he experienced freedom from life's sufferings and found a path for all of us to follow. He said, "May your spiritual journey allow you to accept whatever is happening in your life. This gift of life is your practice. Life itself is your teaching."

July: First Obon service after loved one passes – *Hatsubon*
See the description in the Memorial Services section.

July 15: Obon – Gathering of Joy – *Kangi-e*
Obon is a day to remember those who have gone before us with gratitude for enabling us to exist and to encounter the Dharma. As Shinran observed, "All sentient beings, without exception, have been our parents and brothers and sisters in the course of countless lives in the many states of existence" (*Tannishō*, Chapter 5).

Part of the inspiration for Obon comes from the Ghost Festival of Chinese folk religion, as re-envisioned in a Buddhist context. The word Obon is the shortened form of *urabon-e* which means to suffer as if being hung upside down, and comes from the *Ullambana Sutra*. The sutra tells the story of Maudgalyāyana, one of Śākyamuni Buddha's ten great disciples, and how he suffered over the death of his mother, feeling a deep sense of regret and sorrow. He believed that her devotion to him had been a barrier to her understanding the Dharma. The Buddha told him to reflect upon this, and Maudgalyāyana, known for his deep insight, came to realize that his mother's devotion to him was based on an unselfish love. With this deep insight into his mother's life, he danced with joy as his regret and sorrow were transformed into appreciation and gratitude.

For Shin Buddhists, outdoor folk dancing (*bon odori*) is done in memory of the deceased and not to welcome back the spirits of the departed or to generate merit for them. Thus, it is also called

Gathering of Joy (*Kangi-e*) in grateful remembrance of all those who have influenced our lives.

September 23: Ohigan – Autumn Equinox – *Shūki higan-e*
See "March 21: Ohigan – Spring Equinox."

November: Perpetual Sutras Memorial Service – *Eitaikyō*
Buddhist followers established *Eitaikyō* to continue the teachings for their descendants and to establish a fund for Sangha and temple preservation. So this is customarily a time for monetary gifts to the temple to ensure its future.

Eitaikyō is a contraction of a longer word that means "perpetual *(eitai)* chanting *(doku)* of sutras *(kyō)*." The act of chanting connects us to all those who came before and all those who will follow as we chant these same sutras. We flow together in time, and in the ritual of chanting we become one with them. In this way we endure, and we ourselves are perpetuated, freed from our individual lives.

In some Buddhist traditions, memorial services are performed to accrue merit for deceased loved ones and bring about a favorable rebirth, but Shinran had a different view. He taught that the question of liberation is truly settled for Shin Buddhist followers, and that they realize great, complete nirvāna at the end of *this* life. There is nothing that family and friends need to do to bring about this result. Therefore, *Eitaikyō* is an opportunity for the living to express reverence for the life and actions of those who have died and to make donations for the continuing cultivation of the Dharma.

November: All Life-Forms Service – *Ikitoshi ikerumono no hōyō*
This special service acknowledges our appreciation and gratitude to all forms of life that make our lives possible and enhance our enjoyment. We recognize the countless living forms that sustain and nurture our bodies, as well as the pets who add richness to our lives.

December: Eshinni's and Kakushinni's Memorial

Eshinni and Kakushinni were the wife and daughter of Shinran Shōnin, who are remembered for their support in bringing his teachings to all. Shinran developed the profound insights that are the basis for Shin Buddhism, but he had not intended to start a new school of Buddhism. It is through the efforts of Eshinni and Kakushinni that Shinran's teachings are available to us today.

December 8: Bodhi Day – Buddha's Awakening – *Jōdō-e*

Bodhi is the Sanskrit word for enlightenment. Bodhi Day is when Siddhārtha Gautama became Śākyamuni Buddha. Siddhārtha was 35 when he realized Truth. As a Buddha, he shared the Dharma for 45 years until his death at age 80.

December 31: New Year's Eve – *Joya-e*

The last day of the year is an opportunity to reflect upon the past year in preparation for the coming new year. It is a time to think about the interdependency of all life and to ponder all the causes and conditions that have enabled us to live. At some temples, the bell is struck 108 times to remind us of the 108 blind passions (*bonnō*) that permeate our everyday lives.

Infant Presentation – *Hatsumairi / Shosanshiki*

Parents formally present their child to the Sangha for the first time on this occasion and promise to help them learn the Buddhist path.

Affirmation Rites – *Ti-sarana / Kieshiki*

These are a formal ceremony for those who aspire to follow the Buddhist path by taking refuge in the Three Treasures of the Buddha, Dharma, and Sangha. *Ti-sarana* is for children, and *Kieshiki* is for adults. A formal Dharma name (*hōmyō*) is also given at the *Kieshiki*.

Memorial Services

At specified intervals after a loved one has died, we gather for services to listen to the Dharma. During memorial services, we remember the deceased with gratitude for enabling us to be who we are and to receive the Dharma. It is a time not only to strengthen family ties, but also to reflect upon relationships beyond the immediate family, remembering and appreciating the oneness of all life.

First Obon service after loved one dies – *Hatsubon*
Hatsubon is a service held during the first Obon season after a loved one has died. This is a time to reflect upon our lives and how we are continually being influenced by our loved ones. Because death has so recently touched the *Hatsubon* family and friends, the immediate experience of the impermanence of the physical body leads us to a better understanding that our loved one's life continues to work and influence us.

Monthly Memorial Service – *Shōtsuki hōyō*
Most temples hold a Monthly Memorial Service for all those who died during that particular month of a prior year. The names of the deceased, as recorded in the *Eitaikyō* book of the temple, are read aloud by the minister. Family members and friends then offer incense.

Private Family Memorial Service – *Hōji*
In lieu of attending the *Shōtsuki hōyō*, a family may opt to have a private memorial service or *Hōji*. Arrangements are made with the minister by the family. Traditionally, services for a family member are held on the 7th, 49th, and 100th day, and then one year after the day of death. Thereafter, *Hōji* take place in years 3, 7, 13, 17, 25, 33, 50, and 100 (the day and year of death are counted as 1 in this cycle). The numerical intervals are culturally derived and have no specific meaning in Shin Buddhism. Some families hold a memorial service every year.